Combat Aircraft Library

German
Warplanes
of World War II

Contents

The Luftwaffe's First Weapons   5

Multi-front Nightmare   23

The End of Supremacy   43

Enemy Pressure Grows   57

Defence of the Reich   67

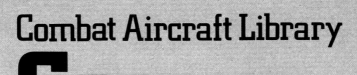

Combat Aircraft Library

German Warplanes

of World War II

Crescent Books
New York

Crescent Books

First English edition published by Temple Press
an imprint of Newnes Books 1983

This edition published by Crescent Books,
a division of Crown Publishers, Inc.
h g f e d c b a

Printed and bound in Italy

Created and produced by Stan Morse
Aerospace Publishing Ltd
10 Barley Mow Passage
London W4 4PH

© Aerospace Publishing Ltd 1983

Colour profiles and line diagrams © Pilot Press Ltd

All correspondence concerning the content of this volume should be addressed to Aerospace
Publishing Ltd. Trade enquiries should be addressed to Crescent Books, New York

ISBN: 0-517-405075

Library of Congress Catalog Card Number: 83-70 128

PICTURE ACKNOWLEDGEMENTS
The publishers would like to thank the following people
and organisations for their help in supplying
photographs for this book.

Jacket front: Military Archive and Research Service
(MARS). **Jacket back:** MARS. **Title page:** John
MacClancy Collection (MacClancy).
5: MARS. **6.** MacClancy. **7:** MacClancy. **8:**
MacClancy. **9:** MacClancy. **14:** MacClancy. **20:**
MacClancy. **22:** MARS. **23:** MARS. **24:** Imperial War
Museum/MacClancy. **25:** Imperial War Museum. **30:**
MacClancy/MARS. **31:** MacClancy. **32:** Bundesarchiv. **33:**
Imperial War Museum. **36:** Bundesarchiv. **38:**
Bundesarchiv. **42:** MARS. **43:** Bundesarchiv. **51:**
Bundesarchiv. **56:** Imperial War Museum. **62:** US Air
Force. **66:** US Air Force. **74:** US Air Force.

THE FIGHTING ECHELONS OF THE LUFTWAFFE

It is perhaps profitable to have a brief explanation of the fighting structure of the Luftwaffe. The basic autonomous and mobile unit was the *Gruppe* (literally group, but equivalent to an RAF Wing) of which there were usually three, and later four in a *Geschwader* (equivalent to an RAF Group). A *Geschwader* of three *Gruppen* was usually established with about 100-120 aircraft, so that each *Gruppe* flew about 30-36 aircraft. The normal tactical flying unit was the *Staffel* (of which the nearest RAF equivalent was the Squadron), comprising about 8-12 aircraft. The *Staffel* was usually commanded by an Oberleutnant or Hauptmann (First Lieutenant or Captain, equivalent to an RAF Flying Officer or Flight Lieutenant), a *Gruppe* by a Major (Major, equivalent to a Squadron Leader), and a *Geschwader* by an Oberstleutnant or Oberst (Lieutenant Colonel or Colonel, equivalent to a Wing Commander or Group Captain). *Staffeln* were denoted by Arabic numerals, and *Gruppen* by Roman characters, 1., 2. and 3. Staffeln being the components of I Gruppe, 4., 5. and 6. Staffeln of II Gruppe, and 7., 8. and 9. Staffeln of III Gruppe.

The *Geschwader* was denoted by its purpose and a number, and this was often suffixed by a courtesy title. Thus II/JG 51 'Mölders' referred to II Gruppe, Jagdgeschwader 'Mölders', and 6./KG 2 'Holzhammer' denoted 6. Staffel (in II Gruppe) of Kampfgeschwader 2 'Wooden Hammer'. Some *Geschwader* (such as Lehrgeschwader 2) comprised a number of specialist *Gruppen*; for instance LG 1 embraced a V Gruppe of *Zerstörer* aircraft, being denoted as V (Z)/LG 1.

All *Geschwader, Gruppen* and *Staffeln* also included about three or four aircraft for use by the CO and staff officers (*Stab*); this was referred to as the *Stabsschwarm*, or in its unit context, the Stab/KG 1 'Hindenburg', Stab II/LG 1 or Stab 4./ZG 26 'Horst Wessel'. The *Stab* included the unit adjutant, technical officer and any other specialist officer attached to the unit.

The Luftwaffe's First Weapons

Germany's air force went to war with highly professional and motivated airmen despite its relatively short existence. Its aircraft had been honed to effectiveness by participation in the Spanish Civil War and, available in large numbers, were among the best in Europe.

When Germany went to war in 1939 she had planned on defeating her European opponents within three years, and determined to do so by overcoming France and the UK before turning against the Soviet Union, thereby avoiding the nightmare situation of facing powerful enemies in the West and East simultaneously. The Luftwaffe was a highly professional force, yet had only been in existence for some six years, and its aircraft, though to some extent tested in the combat conditions of the Spanish Civil War, were regarded as no more than adequate to maintain superiority over other European air forces for those three years.

Moreover, whether or not the Luftwaffe would be able to engage in any sort of strategic air offensive during the three years was highly questionable owing to the fact that plans to create a strategic bomber force had been scrapped in 1936 when Hitler vetoed production of small numbers of large aircraft in favour of much larger production of smaller aircraft. Indeed, unlike the Royal Air Force (which was a wholly self-contained service, independent of the army and navy), the Luftwaffe was largely staffed by ex-army officers who regarded it as an army-support arm

Widely and affectionately known as 'Auntie Junkers', the Ju 52/3m originated as a dual-purpose airliner/bomber design in the early 1930s. It provided almost all the necessary transportation of airborne forces during the German invasions of Poland, Norway, the Low Countries, France and the Balkans.

German Warplanes of World War II

Junkers Ju 87R (S2+MR) of 7./StG 77 during the Balkan campaign of April 1941. This version of the Ju 87, with long range underwing fuel tanks, was first used operationally during the Norwegian campaign a year earlier.

The Ju 87B-1 was the standard version of this notorious dive bomber during the first two years of the war; the example depicted here, 6G+JR, carries the insignia of 7./StG 51 as worn during the Battle of France of May-June 1940.

whose main purpose was to act as a highly mobile artillery and assault force. Long-range bombing, maritime air operations and air-to-air combat were regarded as being almost superfluous in Germany's *Blitzkrieg* (lightning warfare) concept.

Thus when Germany invaded Poland in September 1939, the overwhelming force brought into action in the air comprised large numbers of tactical bombers and ground-support aircraft which could be called down to strike battlefield targets by the army.

Principal among the aircraft flown by the Luftwaffe in 1939 were the Junkers Ju 87 (the famous Stuka) dive-bomber and the Dornier Do 17 medium bomber. With its grotesque, cranked-wing appearance and with sirens attached to its fixed landing gear, the Ju 87 was employed largely as a terror weapon although, provided it faced no fighter opposition, it was used to devastating effect and with great accuracy against small pinpoint targets. It was, however, extremely vulnerable during its steep dive and later came to be regarded as a sitting duck by fighter pilots. The sleek

Junkers Ju 87Bs of StG 77, each carrying a 1,102-lb (500-kg) bomb under the fuselage, on a raid probably during the first two years of the war. In contrast to the RAF's practice of flying close formations, the Luftwaffe preferred the open formation seen here.

This Ju 87B-2 (6G+AC) of Stab II/StG 1 on the Eastern Front late in 1941 wears the temporary winter camouflage of all-over water-soluble white paint. The red eagle insignia on the nose was retained after III/StG 51 was re-designated II/StG 1.

The codes L1+GE identify this Ju 87B as an aircraft of Stab IV (Stuka) Gruppe, Lehrgeschwader 1. This general purpose Geschwader was unusual in possessing five Gruppen with medium bombers, dive bombers and heavy fighters (Zerstörer).

Line-up of Ju 87Bs of Stukageschwader 2 'Immelmann', probably in the Mediterranean theatre during 1941. The nearest two aircraft bear the 'scottie dog' insignia of the Geschwader's II Gruppe.

Dornier Do 17 was an efficient medium bomber by the standards of the time, could carry a useful bomb load of over 2,205 lb (1000 kg) and had a top speed of more than 250 mph (400 km/h). It did display one of the flaws inherent in many German bombers, concentrating all crew members in the nose of the aircraft so that the gunners had many blind spots in their fields of fire.

The Heinkel He 111 was less vulnerable in this respect. This excellent heavy bomber had also received its baptism of fire in Spain in its early forms, but the much improved He 111P was only reaching the Luftwaffe in significant numbers when German troops marched into Poland. Capable of carrying a bomb load of about 4,409 lb (2000 kg) and possessing a top speed of nearly 250 mph (400 km/h), the He 111 was certainly one of the best heavy bombers in Europe in 1939-40 and, with a defensive armament of six machine-guns, was able to put up a respectable defence against most contemporary fighters. It was the He 111 that carried out the devastating and widely criticized raids on Warsaw and Rotterdam during the first year of the war, bringing to reality the concept of total war.

German Warplanes of World War II

First production version of the Dornier Do 17 bomber was the Do 17E-1, of which a small number was delivered to the Legion Cóndor serving in Spain with the Nationalist Forces in 1937; it had however been relegated to second-line duties with the Luftwaffe by September 1939.

Another bomber that was just beginning to join the Luftwaffe in September 1939 was the superb Junkers Ju 88, often mistakenly regarded as a dive-bomber on account of the dive-brakes fitted under the wings, but in fact a fast medium bomber whose attacks were frequently carried out in a shallow dive from medium or low level. Able to carry a 2,205-lb (1000-kg) bombload, the early Ju 88 had a top speed of nearly 300 mph (480 km/h), as fast as or faster than half the fighters in service with European air forces.

Blitzkrieg

The Luftwaffe's fighter arm (the *Jagdverband*) had standardized on a single aircraft, the brilliant Messerschmitt Bf 109, a small, fast and highly manoeuvrable single-seater that was more than a match for any opponent that Germany expected to meet early in the war. If it earned any criticism it was for its poor armament, which certainly fell short of RAF Fighter Command's eight-gun batteries in the Hawker Hurricane and Supermarine Spitfire. No one could foresee that the war would drag on for six years, or that the Bf 109 would fight right up to the last day, would destroy more enemy aircraft than any other and would be produced in greater numbers than any other aircraft in the world.

Despite the lack of a strategic bombing force, already mentioned, Germany went to war with a well-balanced range of combat aircraft and, in some respects, its operational concepts were less

At the outbreak of war the Dornier Do 17P had also almost disappeared from operational service, only 83 such aircraft remaining on Luftwaffe charge on 2 September 1939. The aircraft, seen here during the winter of 1939-40, belong to KG 3 'Blitz-Geschwader'.

A Dornier Do 17Z of 4. Staffel, Kampfgeschwader 2 'Holzhammer', based at Arras in 1940. The Do 17 was the least efficient of the Luftwaffe's Do 17/ He 111/Ju 88 bomber trio and by 1941 was being withdrawn from front line service.

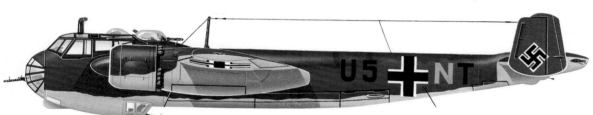

KG 2 started receiving the improved Do 217E in 1941, this E-2 bearing the codes of the Geschwader's 9. Staffel. This version introduced an electrically-operated dorsal turret with single 13-mm (0.51-in) machine-gun; some aircraft, as here, mounted four machine-guns in the tail cone.

constricted by traditional ideas than among her opponents. The Luftwaffe had, for example, evolved a radical type of heavy fighter, or *Zerstörer* (destroyer), of which the new Messerschmitt Bf 110 was the first and had entered service shortly before the war. Possessing a top speed of over 350 mph (560 km/h) and heavy armament, this fighter was regarded as a devastating weapon; while regarded as the brainchild of Hermann Goering himself, the *Zerstörergeschwader* (destroyer wings) were hailed as the elite arm of the Luftwaffe, on a par with the army generals' favourite, the *Stukageschwader* (diver-bomber wings); perhaps it was no accident that many of their crews contained Goering's fellow Prussian gentry.

Among the supporting aircraft were the rugged three-engine Junkers Ju 52/3m troop transports (affectionately known as 'Tante Ju', or Auntie Junkers), developed directly from a civil airliner; the four-engine Focke-Wulf Fw 200 Condor, also a former airliner which came to be adapted for military purposes, this time for maritime reconnaissance; the Henschel Hs 126, a short range reconnaissance aircraft with short take-off performance and used for battlefield surveillance, and a vital element of the *Blitzkrieg* tactic; the Dornier Do 18 flying-boat and Heinkel He 59 coastal reconnaissance floatplane; and the Heinkel He 115 minelaying floatplane.

This then was Germany's air arsenal, a powerful and well-balanced range of excellent aircraft, flown by well-trained, professional and dedicated crews, and supplied by an efficient manufacturing industry fairly well dispersed throughout the German hinterland.

All went well for the Luftwaffe during the first eight months of the war. Poland was crushed

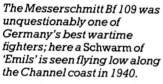

The Messerschmitt Bf 109 was unquestionably one of Germany's best wartime fighters; here a Schwarm of 'Emils' is seen flying low along the Channel coast in 1940.

The Messerschmitt Bf 109E-7 was introduced during the latter stages of the Battle of Britain, capable of carrying an underfuselage drop tank so as to provide fighter escort for German bombers. The aircraft shown belonged to Lehrgeschwader 2, and was shot down over London on 15 September 1940.

Messerschmitt Bf 109

History and Notes

First flown in September 1935, Willy Messerschmitt's single-seat Bf 109 fighter saw action during the Spanish Civil War in the Bf 109B series version (Junkers Jumo 210 engine), joining the Luftwaffe in 1937 and being followed by the Bf 109C with armament increased from three to four rifle-calibre machine-guns. The Bf 109D introduced the Daimler-Benz DB 600 engine and hub-firing cannon, and was produced in 1938-9.

First major production variant was the Bf 109E with DB 601E engine and direct fuel-injection, and variations of armament between two machine-guns, and four machine-guns and one hub-cannon. Fighter-bomber and reconnaissance versions were produced during 1940. The Bf 109E was the Luftwaffe's principal fighter during 1939-40. It was followed by the Bf 109F, powered initially by the DB 601N and later the DB 601E, and introduced such equipment as nitrous-oxide power boosting, faster-firing guns (15-mm MG 151) and optional underwing gun pods. Both the Bf 109E and Bf 109F existed in tropicalized form for service in North Africa during 1941-2.

The Bf 109G, with DB 605 engine, served from 1942 until 1945 on all fronts, being built in the largest numbers and introducing armament variations which included 30-mm guns. Fastest of all was the Bf 109 G-10 (429 mph/90 km/h). Final main production version was the Bf 109K with boosted versions of the DB 605. Other versions included the Bf 109H high-altitude fighter and Bf 109T shipboard fighter.

More than 33,000 Bf 109s were built between 1937 and 1945.

Specification: Messerschmitt Bf 109G-6
Origin: Germany
Type: single-seat interceptor fighter
Powerplant: one 1,476-hp (1100-kW) Daimler-Benz DB 605A inline piston engine
Performance: maximum speed 387 mph (623 km/h) at 22,965 ft (7000 m); climb to 19,685 ft (6000 m) in 6.0 minutes; service ceiling 38,550 ft (11750 m); normal range 450 miles (725 km)
Weights: empty 5,952 lb (2700 kg); maximum take-off 6,944 lb (3150 kg)
Dimensions: span 32 ft 6½ in (9.92 m); length 29 ft 7 in (9.02 m); height 11 ft 2 in (3.40 m); wing area 172.8 sq ft (16.05 m²)
Armament: two nose-mounted 7.92-mm (0.31-in) MG 151/20 cannon guns, one 30-mm MK 108 cannon firing through propeller hub and two 20-mm MG 151/20 cannon mounted under the wings

Keith Fretwell.

German Warplanes of World War II

By 1940 the Bf 109C had been withdrawn as a day fighter, but was reintroduced as a makeshift night fighter that year, this aircraft serving with 10.(Nacht)/JG 77 interim night fighter Staffel, based at Aalborg, Denmark, in July.

Bf 109E-3 of Adolf Galland's unit 9./JG 26, based at Caffiers, France in August 1940.

Wearing the insignia of a Gruppenkommandeur, this Bf 109E-3 was flown by Hauptmann Hentschel of II Gruppe, Jagdgeschwader 77, based at Stavanger and Trondheim, Norway, during the period of the Battle of Britain.

Messerschmitt Bf 109E-4

1 Hollow propeller hub
2 Spinner
3 Three-blade VDM variable-pitch propeller
4 Propeller pitch-change mechanism
5 Spinner back plate
6 Glycol coolant header tank
7 Glycol filler cap
8 Cowling fastener
9 Chin intake
10 Coolant pipe fairing
11 Exhaust forward fairing
12 Additional (long-range) oil tank
13 Daimler-Benz DB 601A engine
14 Supplementary intakes
15 Fuselage machine-gun troughs
16 Anti-vibration engine mounting pads
17 Exhaust ejector stubs

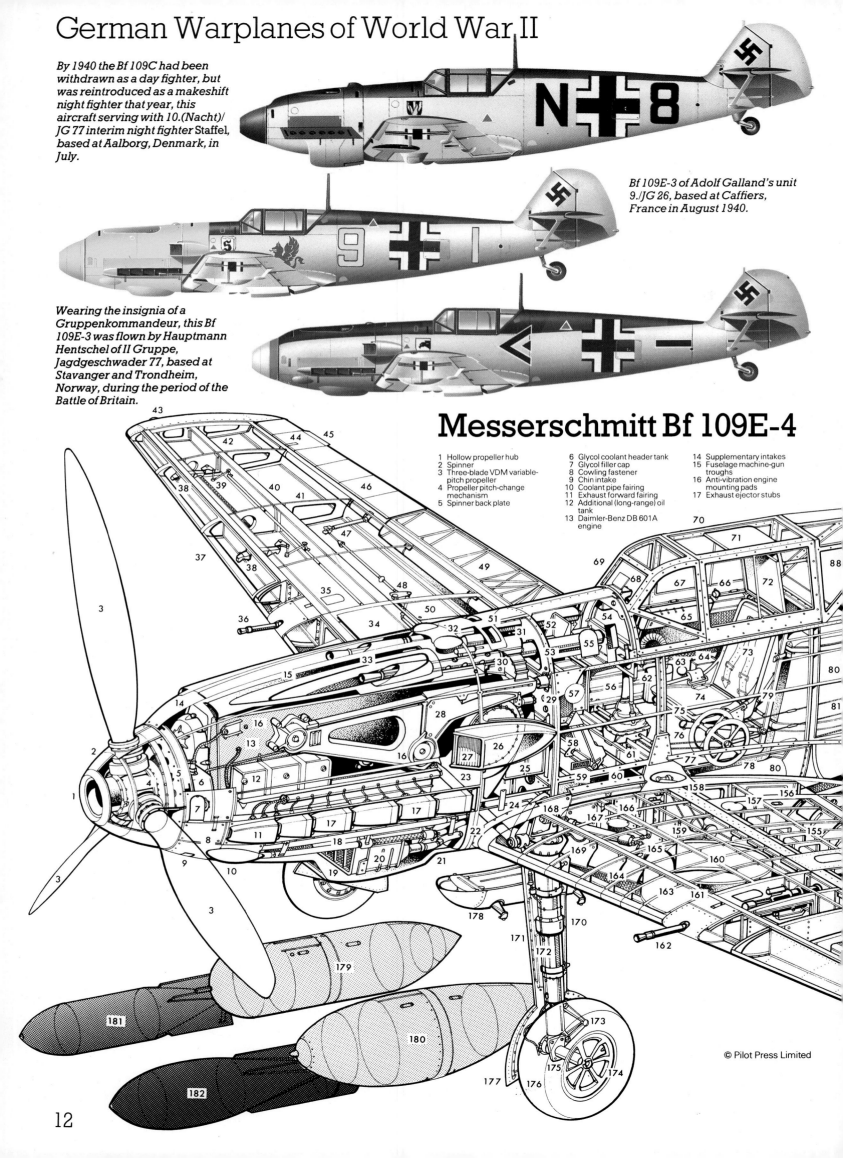

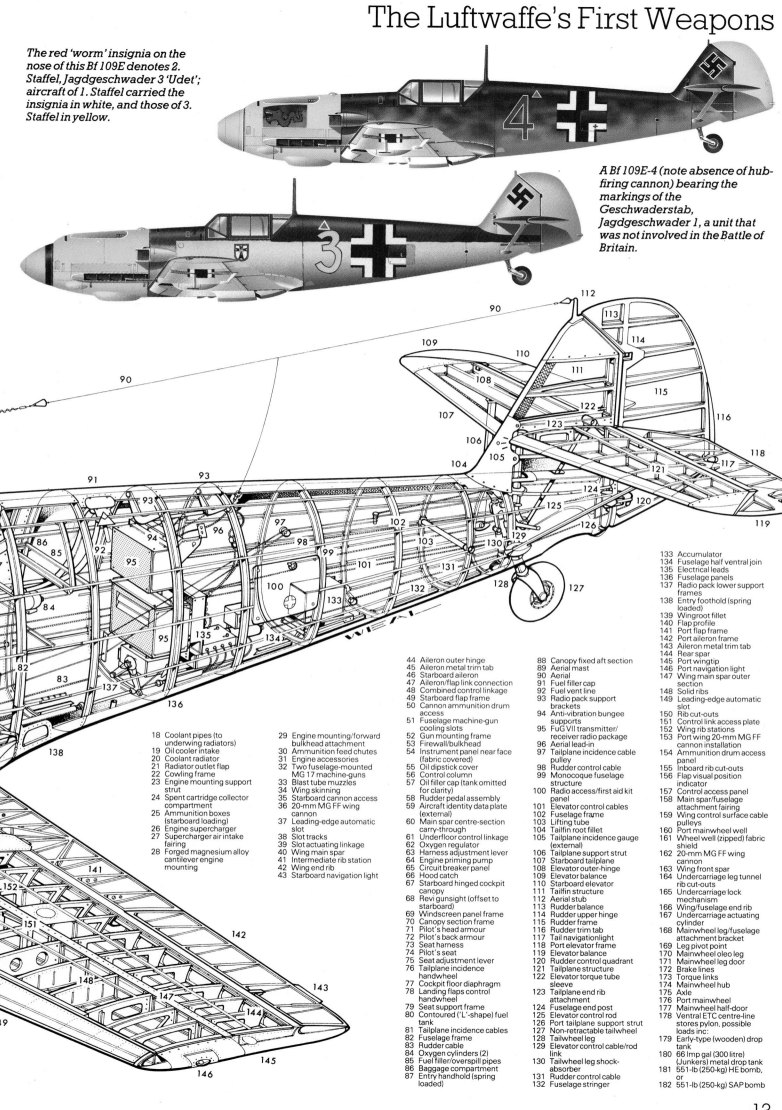

The red 'worm' insignia on the nose of this Bf 109E denotes 2. Staffel, Jagdgeschwader 3 'Udet'; aircraft of 1. Staffel carried the insignia in white, and those of 3. Staffel in yellow.

A Bf 109E-4 (note absence of hub-firing cannon) bearing the markings of the Geschwaderstab, Jagdgeschwader 1, a unit that was not involved in the Battle of Britain.

18 Coolant pipes (to underwing radiators)
19 Oil cooler intake
20 Coolant radiator
21 Radiator outlet flap
22 Cowling frame
23 Engine mounting support strut
24 Spent cartridge collector compartment
25 Ammunition boxes (starboard loading)
26 Engine supercharger
27 Supercharger air intake fairing
28 Forged magnesium alloy cantilever engine mounting
29 Engine mounting/forward bulkhead attachment
30 Ammunition feed chutes
31 Engine accessories
32 Two fuselage-mounted MG 17 machine-guns
33 Blast tube muzzles
34 Wing skinning
35 Starboard cannon access
36 20-mm MG FF wing cannon
37 Leading-edge automatic slot
38 Slot tracks
39 Slot actuating linkage
40 Wing main spar
41 Intermediate rib station
42 Wing end rib
43 Starboard navigation light
44 Aileron outer hinge
45 Aileron metal trim tab
46 Starboard aileron
47 Aileron/flap link connection
48 Combined control linkage
49 Starboard flap frame
50 Cannon ammunition drum access
51 Fuselage machine-gun cooling slots
52 Gun mounting frame
53 Firewall/bulkhead
54 Instrument panel near face (fabric covered)
55 Oil dipstick cover
56 Control column
57 Oil filler cap (tank omitted for clarity)
58 Rudder pedal assembly
59 Aircraft identity data plate (external)
60 Main spar centre-section carry-through
61 Underfloor control linkage
62 Oxygen regulator
63 Harness adjustment lever
64 Engine priming pump
65 Circuit breaker panel
66 Hood catch
67 Starboard hinged cockpit canopy
68 Revi gunsight (offset to starboard)
69 Windscreen panel frame
70 Canopy section frame
71 Pilot's head armour
72 Pilot's back armour
73 Seat harness
74 Pilot's seat
75 Seat adjustment lever
76 Tailplane incidence handwheel
77 Cockpit floor diaphragm
78 Landing flaps control handwheel
79 Seat support frame
80 Contoured ('L'-shape) fuel tank
81 Tailplane incidence cables
82 Fuselage frame
83 Rudder cable
84 Oxygen cylinders (2)
85 Fuel filler/overspill pipes
86 Baggage compartment
87 Entry handhold (spring loaded)
88 Canopy fixed aft section
89 Aerial mast
90 Aerial
91 Fuel filler cap
92 Fuel vent line
93 Radio pack support brackets
94 Anti-vibration bungee supports
95 FuG VII transmitter/ receiver radio package
96 Aerial lead-in
97 Tailplane incidence cable pulley
98 Rudder control cable
99 Monocoque fuselage structure
100 Radio access/first aid kit panel
101 Elevator control cables
102 Fuselage frame
103 Lifting tube
104 Tailfin root fillet
105 Tailplane incidence gauge (external)
106 Tailplane support strut
107 Starboard tailplane
108 Elevator outer-hinge
109 Elevator balance
110 Starboard elevator
111 Tailfin structure
112 Aerial stub
113 Rudder balance
114 Rudder upper hinge
115 Rudder frame
116 Rudder trim tab
117 Tail navigation light
118 Port elevator frame
119 Elevator balance
120 Rudder control quadrant
121 Tailplane structure
122 Elevator torque tube sleeve
123 Tailplane end rib attachment
124 Tailplane end post
125 Elevator control rod
126 Port tailplane support strut
127 Non-retractable tailwheel
128 Tailwheel leg
129 Elevator control cable/rod link
130 Tailwheel leg shock-absorber
131 Rudder control cable
132 Fuselage stringer
133 Accumulator
134 Fuselage half ventral join
135 Electrical leads
136 Fuselage panels
137 Radio pack lower support frames
138 Entry foothold (spring loaded)
139 Wingroot fillet
140 Flap profile
141 Port flap frame
142 Port aileron frame
143 Aileron metal trim tab
144 Rear spar
145 Port wingtip
146 Port navigation light
147 Wing main spar outer section
148 Solid ribs
149 Leading-edge automatic slot
150 Rib cut-outs
151 Control link access plate
152 Wing rib stations
153 Port wing 20-mm MG FF cannon installation
154 Ammunition drum access panel
155 Inboard rib cut-outs
156 Flap visual position indicator
157 Control access panel
158 Main spar/fuselage attachment fairing
159 Wing control surface cable pulleys
160 Port mainwheel well
161 Wheel well (zipped) fabric shield
162 20-mm MG FF wing cannon
163 Wing front spar
164 Undercarriage leg tunnel rib cut-outs
165 Undercarriage lock mechanism
166 Wing/fuselage end rib
167 Undercarriage actuating cylinder
168 Mainwheel leg/fuselage attachment bracket
169 Leg pivot point
170 Mainwheel oleo leg
171 Mainwheel leg door
172 Brake lines
173 Torque links
174 Mainwheel hub
175 Axle
176 Port mainwheel
177 Mainwheel half-door
178 Ventral ETC centre-line stores pylon, possible loads inc:
179 Early-type (wooden) drop tank
180 66 Imp gal (300 litre) (Junkers) metal drop tank
181 551-lb (250-kg) HE bomb, or
182 551-lb (250-kg) SAP bomb

German Warplanes of World War II

Bearing the distinctive wasp device on its nose, this Messerschmitt Bf 110C-4/B (G9+1N) served with 5. Staffel, Zerstörergeschwader 1 'Wespen Geschwader', in the Caucasus during October 1942.

despite a gallant but forlorn resistance by her outmoded air force. In truth the Luftwaffe was scarcely extended, and the campaign served only to feed the myth of *Blitzkrieg* invincibility. The dive-bombers attacked without serious intervention by opposing fighters, and the Heinkels achieved suitably impressive devastation in the sprawling capital of Warsaw. And the campaign was concluded in less than a month.

Occupation of Europe

The Norwegian campaign, though always a lost cause for the UK, posed its own problems for the Luftwaffe, not least of which were the distances involved and the relative absence of airfields. Ju 52/3m transports were used to land airborne forces at key points in the south of the country while the Bf 110s were the only available fighters with adequate range to provide cover. Only in the final stages of the campaign was the Luftwaffe given a foretaste of things to come when, in the far north, unescorted bombers and transports faced the modern Hurricane fighters of the RAF, and suffered accordingly.

Before the Norwegian campaign drew to its inevitable end, the great German attack in the West had been launched on 10 May, the full panoply of *Blitzkrieg* armoury and tactics being unleashed on France and the Low Countries. For a period of about one week the Luftwaffe was fighting the combined air forces of the UK, France, the Netherlands and Belgium. Every conceivable type of German military aircraft was given a specific role. He 111s rained bombs on Rotterdam as Do 17s roamed the skies over French airfields; Ju 87s struck at targets in the path of the advancing German army as Bf 110s flew top cover; Bf 109s decimated the Dutch and Belgian air forces as Ju 52/3ms poured airborne forces into key objectives in the Low Countries, and Ju 88s struck at targets on the Belgian coast. In a number of 'set-piece' attacks novel tactics were employed: a dozen He 59 biplanes alighted on the Maas river, bringing 120 troops to capture the key bridge at Rotterdam; DFS 230 gliders landed with assault troops on the key Belgian fort of Eben Emael. And all the while the Hs 126 reconnaissance aircraft buzzed to and fro over the rumbling *Panzer* forces.

A pair of Bf 110C-2s of 1./ZG 52, based in June 1940 at Charleville during the Battle of France. Though fast and well-armed, the Bf 110 proved extremely vulnerable in the presence of nimble single-seat interceptor fighters.

Junkers Ju 52

History and Notes

Affectionately known throughout the German forces as *Tante Ju* (Auntie Junkers) the three-engine Ju 52/3m with characteristic corrugated metal skin was widely used as a pre-war commercial airliner before being employed, first as a bomber and later as a troop transport, by the Luftwaffe. The Ju 52/3mg3e was flown in both roles by the Legion Cóndor in Spain from 1936 onwards. On the eve of the invasion of Poland the Luftwaffe fielded 552 transports, of which no fewer than 547 were Ju 52/3ms (the Ju 52/3mg4e and Ju52/3mg5e versions, these aircraft having provision for alternative wheel, float or ski landing gear). Improved radio identified the Ju 52/3mg6e, and one of the main production versions, the Ju 52/3mg7e, featured automatic pilot, wider loading doors and accommodation for 18 assault troops. The Ju 52/3mg8e introduced increased cabin windows and a 13-mm (0.51-in) machine-gun in a dorsal position, and the Ju 52/3mg9e glider tug was stressed for increased take-off weight. The Ju 52/3mg10e was powered by BMW 132L radials. The final version, introduced late in 1943 when Allied fighters posed a greatly increased threat in all theatres, featured a 7.92-mm (0.31-in) gun over the cockpit. Estimates of total Ju 52/3m production (in Germany and elsewhere) vary between 5,600 and 5,900. Famous battles and campaigns in which the sturdy old workhorse participated included Norway, Crete, Demyansk (where some 200 Ju 52/3ms airlifted 24,000 tons of relief supplies, 15,000 troops and 20,000 casualties in three months), Stalingrad and Tunisia.

Specification: Junkers Ju 52/3mg4e
Origin: Germany
Type: two/three-crew 18-seat military transport
Powerplant: three 830-hp (619-kW) BMW 132T radial piston engines

A Junkers Ju 52/3m (1Z+AF) of IV Gruppe, Kampfgeschwader zur besonderen Verwendung 1 (KGzbV 1). The splinter camouflage shown here was not widely adopted.

Performance: maximum speed 168 mph (270 km/h) at sea level; initial climb rate 689 ft (210 m) per minute; service ceiling 18,045 ft (5500 m); range 570 miles (917 km)
Weights: empty 14,352 lb (6510 kg); maximum take-off 23,148 lb (10500 kg)
Dimensions: span 95 ft 11½ in (29.25 m); length 62 ft 0 in (18.90 m); height 11 ft 9¾ in (3.60 m); wing area 1,189.5 sq ft (110.50 m²)
Accommodation: 16 fully-equipped assault troops or 18 parachute troops; when specially adapted as air ambulance, 12 stretcher cases

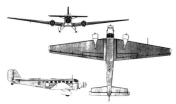

Junkers Ju 52/3mge

The Junkers Ju 52/3m proved robust and reliable in Luftwaffe service. More important, it was readily available.

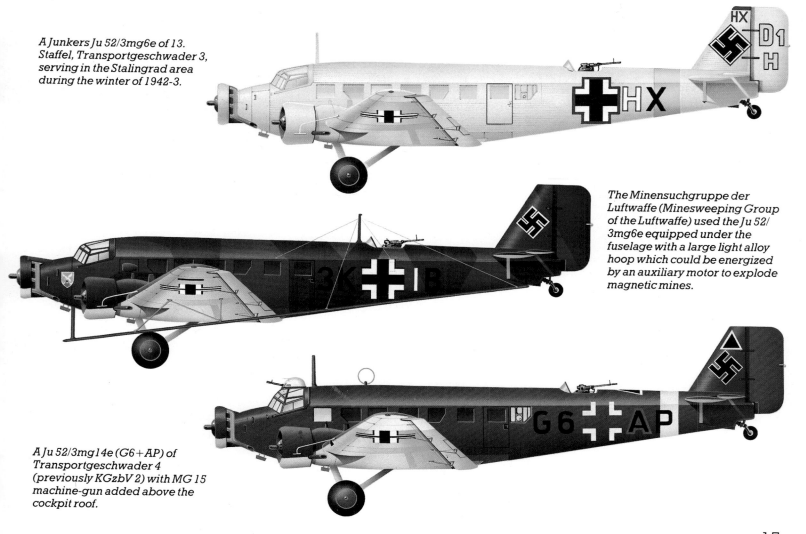

A Junkers Ju 52/3mg6e of 13. Staffel, Transportgeschwader 3, serving in the Stalingrad area during the winter of 1942-3.

The Minensuchgruppe der Luftwaffe (Minesweeping Group of the Luftwaffe) used the Ju 52/3mg6e equipped under the fuselage with a large light alloy hoop which could be energized by an auxiliary motor to explode magnetic mines.

A Ju 52/3mg14e (G6+AP) of Transportgeschwader 4 (previously KGzbV 2) with MG 15 machine-gun added above the cockpit roof.

German Warplanes of World War II

Messerschmitt Bf 110C-4/B of 9. Staffel, Zerstörergeschwader 26 'Horst Wessel', shown carrying two 551-lb (250-kg) and four 220-lb (100-kg) bombs. This unit was among the first German units to be sent to the Mediterranean, being based at Palermo at the end of 1940.

Messerschmitt Bf 110

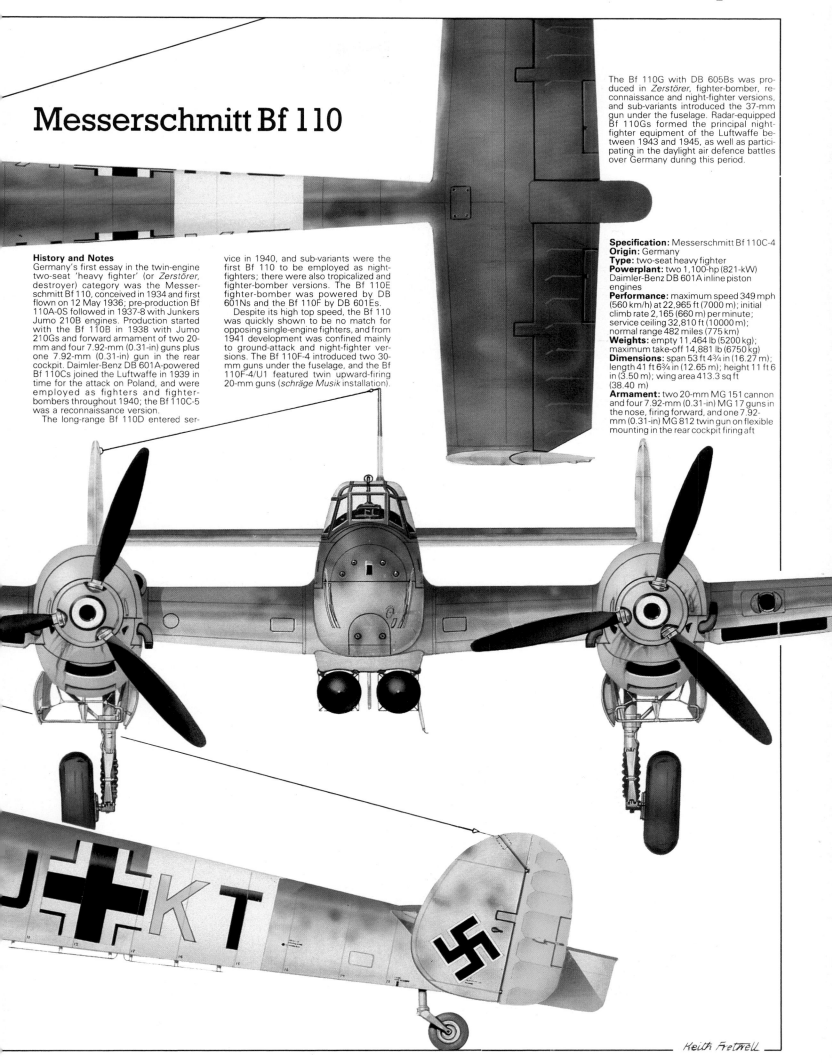

The Bf 110G with DB 605Bs was produced in *Zerstörer*, fighter-bomber, reconnaissance and night-fighter versions, and sub-variants introduced the 37-mm gun under the fuselage. Radar-equipped Bf 110Gs formed the principal night-fighter equipment of the Luftwaffe between 1943 and 1945, as well as participating in the daylight air defence battles over Germany during this period.

History and Notes
Germany's first essay in the twin-engine two-seat 'heavy fighter' (or *Zerstörer*, destroyer) category was the Messerschmitt Bf 110, conceived in 1934 and first flown on 12 May 1936; pre-production Bf 110A-0S followed in 1937-8 with Junkers Jumo 210B engines. Production started with the Bf 110B in 1938 with Jumo 210Gs and forward armament of two 20-mm and four 7.92-mm (0.31-in) guns plus one 7.92-mm (0.31-in) gun in the rear cockpit. Daimler-Benz DB 601A-powered Bf 110Cs joined the Luftwaffe in 1939 in time for the attack on Poland, and were employed as fighters and fighter-bombers throughout 1940; the Bf 110C-5 was a reconnaissance version.

The long-range Bf 110D entered service in 1940, and sub-variants were the first Bf 110 to be employed as night-fighters; there were also tropicalized and fighter-bomber versions. The Bf 110E fighter-bomber was powered by DB 601Ns and the Bf 110F by DB 601Es.

Despite its high top speed, the Bf 110 was quickly shown to be no match for opposing single-engine fighters, and from 1941 development was confined mainly to ground-attack and night-fighter versions. The Bf 110F-4 introduced two 30-mm guns under the fuselage, and the Bf 110F-4/U1 featured twin upward-firing 20-mm guns (*schräge Musik* installation).

Specification: Messerschmitt Bf 110C-4
Origin: Germany
Type: two-seat heavy fighter
Powerplant: two 1,100-hp (821-kW) Daimler-Benz DB 601A inline piston engines
Performance: maximum speed 349 mph (560 km/h) at 22,965 ft (7000 m); initial climb rate 2,165 (660 m) per minute; service ceiling 32,810 ft (10000 m); normal range 482 miles (775 km)
Weights: empty 11,464 lb (5200 kg); maximum take-off 14,881 lb (6750 kg)
Dimensions: span 53 ft 4¾ in (16.27 m); length 41 ft 6¾ in (12.65 m); height 11 ft 6 in (3.50 m); wing area 413.3 sq ft (38.40 m)
Armament: two 20-mm MG 151 cannon and four 7.92-mm (0.31-in) MG 17 guns in the nose, firing forward, and one 7.92-mm (0.31-in) MG 812 twin gun on flexible mounting in the rear cockpit firing aft

Keith Fretwell

German Warplanes of World War II

The Messerschmitt Bf 110 (shown here in the markings of 2. Staffel, Zerstörergeschwader 26 'Horst Wessel') proved a disappointment in the daylight operations over Britain in the summer of 1940, lacking the manoeuvrability needed to combat British interceptors; eventually it had to be provided with its own fighter cover.

A Bf 110C-4/B of Schnellkampfgeschwader 210 (SKG 210, fast bomber wing) over the Eastern Front. This unit had originated as Erprobungsgruppe 210 in 1940 but became ZG 1 'Wespen Geschwader' later, before becoming SKG 210; the aircraft shown retains ZG 1's wasp markings on the nose.

Messerschmitt Bf 110G-4b/R3

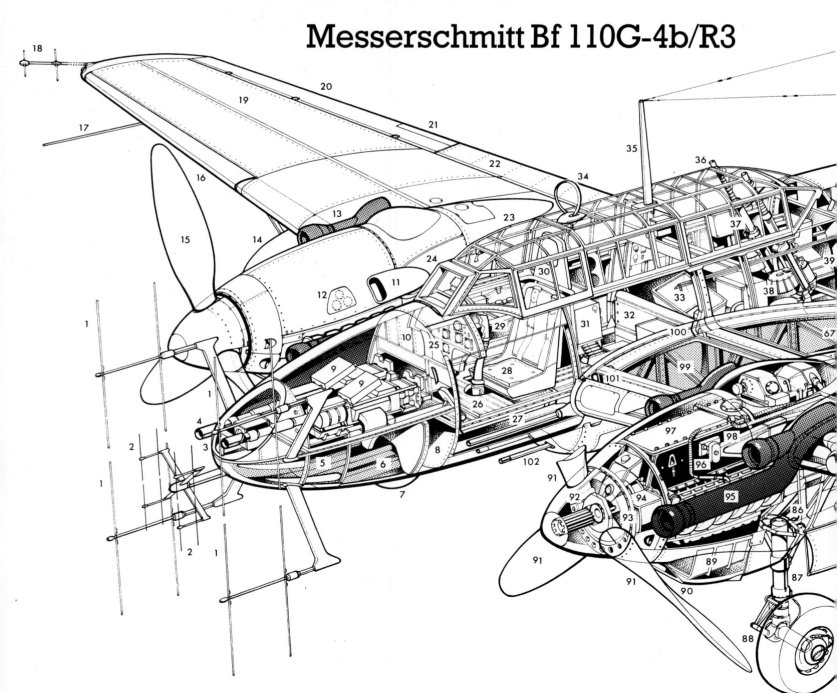

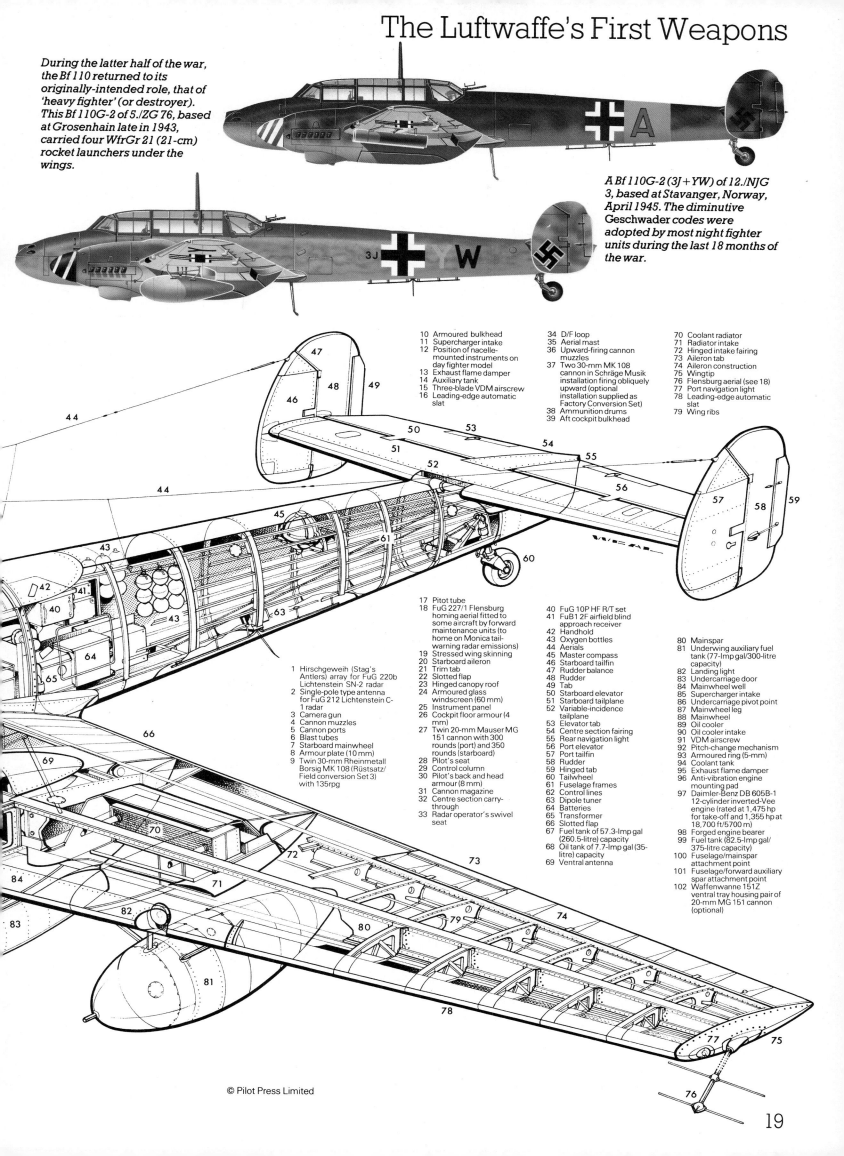

The Luftwaffe's First Weapons

During the latter half of the war, the Bf 110 returned to its originally-intended role, that of 'heavy fighter' (or destroyer). This Bf 110G-2 of 5./ZG 76, based at Grosenhain late in 1943, carried four WfrGr 21 (21-cm) rocket launchers under the wings.

A Bf 110G-2 (3J+YW) of 12./NJG 3, based at Stavanger, Norway, April 1945. The diminutive Geschwader codes were adopted by most night fighter units during the last 18 months of the war.

1 Hirschgeweih (Stag's Antlers) array for FuG 220b Lichtenstein SN-2 radar
2 Single-pole type antenna for FuG 212 Lichtenstein C-1 radar
3 Camera gun
4 Cannon muzzles
5 Cannon ports
6 Blast tubes
7 Starboard mainwheel
8 Armour plate (10 mm)
9 Twin 30-mm Rheinmetall Borsig MK 108 (Rüstsatz/Field conversion Set 3) with 135rpg
10 Armoured bulkhead
11 Supercharger intake
12 Position of nacelle-mounted instruments on day fighter model
13 Exhaust flame damper
14 Auxiliary tank
15 Three-blade VDM airscrew
16 Leading-edge automatic slat
17 Pitot tube
18 FuG 227/1 Flensburg homing aerial fitted to some aircraft by forward maintenance units (to home on Monica tail-warning radar emissions)
19 Stressed wing skinning
20 Starboard aileron
21 Trim tab
22 Slotted flap
23 Hinged canopy roof
24 Armoured glass windscreen (60 mm)
25 Instrument panel
26 Cockpit floor armour (4 mm)
27 Twin 20-mm Mauser MG 151 cannon with 300 rounds (port) and 350 rounds (starboard)
28 Pilot's seat
29 Control column
30 Pilot's back and head armour (8 mm)
31 Cannon magazine
32 Centre section carry-through
33 Radar operator's swivel seat
34 D/F loop
35 Aerial mast
36 Upward-firing cannon muzzles
37 Two 30-mm MK 108 cannon in Schräge Musik installation firing obliquely upward (optional installation supplied as Factory Conversion Set)
38 Ammunition drums
39 Aft cockpit bulkhead
40 FuG 10P HF R/T set
41 FuB1 2F airfield blind approach receiver
42 Handhold
43 Oxygen bottles
44 Aerials
45 Master compass
46 Starboard tailfin
47 Rudder balance
48 Rudder
49 Tab
50 Starboard elevator
51 Starboard tailplane
52 Variable-incidence tailplane
53 Elevator tab
54 Centre section fairing
55 Rear navigation light
56 Port elevator
57 Port tailfin
58 Rudder
59 Hinged tab
60 Tailwheel
61 Fuselage frames
62 Control lines
63 Dipole tuner
64 Batteries
65 Transformer
66 Slotted flap
67 Fuel tank of 57.3-Imp gal (260.5-litre) capacity
68 Oil tank of 7.7-Imp gal (35-litre) capacity
69 Ventral antenna
70 Coolant radiator
71 Radiator intake
72 Hinged intake fairing
73 Aileron tab
74 Aileron construction
75 Wingtip
76 Flensburg aerial (see 18)
77 Port navigation light
78 Leading-edge automatic slat
79 Wing ribs
80 Mainspar
81 Underwing auxiliary fuel tank (77-Imp gal/300-litre capacity)
82 Landing light
83 Undercarriage door
84 Mainwheel well
85 Supercharger intake
86 Undercarriage pivot point
87 Mainwheel leg
88 Mainwheel
89 Oil cooler
90 Oil cooler intake
91 VDM airscrew
92 Pitch-change mechanism
93 Armoured ring (5-mm)
94 Coolant tank
95 Exhaust flame damper
96 Anti-vibration engine mounting pad
97 Daimler-Benz DB 605B-1 12-cylinder inverted-Vee engine (rated at 1,475 hp for take-off and 1,355 hp at 18,700 ft/5700 m)
98 Forged engine bearer
99 Fuel tank (82.5-Imp gal/375-litre capacity)
100 Fuselage/mainspar attachment point
101 Fuselage/forward auxiliary spar attachment point
102 Waffenwanne 151Z ventral tray housing pair of 20-mm MG 151 cannon (optional)

Focke-Wulf Fw 200 Condor

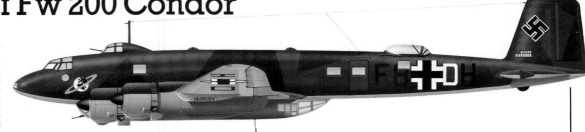

History and Notes

Famous as a pre-war airliner with a number of formidable long-distance flights and records to its credit, the four-engine Focke-Wulf Fw 200 Condor was designed by Kurt Tank in 1936, and underwent military adaptation into a fairly potent anti-shipping aircraft with the Luftwaffe. Ten pre-production Fw 200C-0 maritime reconnaissance aircraft were delivered to the Luftwaffe in September 1939, some of them serving with I./KG 40 in 1940. The five-crew production Fw 200C-1 was powered by four 830-hp (619-kW) BMW 132H engines, was armed with a 20-mm gun in the nose and three 7.92-mm (0.31-in) guns in other positions, and could carry four 551-lb (250-kg) bombs. Apart from long-range maritime patrols over the Atlantic, the F2 200C-1s also undertook extensive minelaying in British waters during 1940, each carrying two 2,205-lb (1000-kg) mines. Numerous sub-variants of the C-series appeared, of which the Fw 200C-3 with 1,000-hp (746-kW) Bramo 323R-2 radials was the most important. Later in the war the Fw 200C-6 and Fw 200C-8 were produced in an effort to enhance the Condor's operational potential by adaptation to carry two Henschel Hs 293 missiles in conjunction with FuG 203b missile control radio.

Rugged operating conditions highlighted the Fw 200's numerous structural weaknesses and there were numerous accidents in service, and for a short time in the mid-war years Fw 200s were employed as military transports, 18 aircraft being flown by Kampfgruppe zur besonderen Verwendung 200 in support of the beleaguered German forces at Stalingrad. Other Condors were used by Hitler and Himmler as personal transports. Focke-Wulf Fw 200 production for the Luftwaffe amounted to 252 aircraft between 1940 and 1944.

This Fw 200 (F8+DH) of 1. Staffel was based at Bordeaux-Mérignac late in 1940 for maritime operations over Britain's Western Approaches.

Specification: Focke-Wulf Fw 200 C-3/U4
Origin: Germany
Type: seven-crew long-range maritime reconnaissance bomber
Powerplant: four 1,000-hp (746-kW) BMW-Bramo 323R-2 radial piston engines
Performance: maximum speed 224 mph (360 km/h) at 15,420 ft (4700 m); service ceiling 19,685 ft (6000 m); range 2,211 miles (3560 km)
Weights: empty 37,478 lb (17000 kg); maximum take-off 50,044 lb (22700 kg)
Dimensions: span 107 ft 9½ in (32.84 m); length 76 ft 11½ in (23.85 m); height 20 ft 8 in (6.30 m); wing area 1,290.0 sq ft (118.00 m²)
Armament: one 7.92-mm (0.31-in) gun in forward dorsal turret, one 13-mm (0.51-in) gun in rear dorsal position, two 13-mm (0.51-in) guns in beam positions, one 20-mm gun in forward position of ventral gondola and one 7.92-mm (0.31-in) gun in aft ventral position, plus a maximum bomb load of 4,630 lb (2100 kg)

Focke-Wulf Fw 200C-8/U10

The Fw 200C-3/U2, which entered Luftwaffe service in 1941, introduced a Lotfe 7D bombsight, but featured reduced gun armament.

Within a week the Netherlands had been overrun, and Belgium followed 10 days later. France eventually collapsed in mid-June, her air force unable to blunt the thrusts of *Blitzkrieg* and being constantly forced to abandon its poorly prepared airfields. In the north of the country, as the UK tried desperately to recover her battered army from Dunkirk, the Luftwaffe was forced into its first major and prolonged air battle against a modern fighter force. While the German air fighting tactics proved superior to those of the RAF, the bombers were suddenly found to be surprisingly vulnerable to the onslaughts of determined fighter pilots in modern aircraft. The much-vaunted Ju 87 was seen to be particularly brittle in the rough-house mêlée with enemy fighters; even the Bf 110 was seen to be a ponderous weapon in the presence of British fighters. The British, on the other hand, found the German aircraft to be rugged in combat, demanding much more than fleeting hits

Refuelling an Fw 200C-3 of 2. Staffel, Kampfgeschwader 40. Normally based at Bordeaux-Mérignac, France, these aircraft were detached to the Stalingrad front during the winter of 1942-3 for use as bomber-transports.

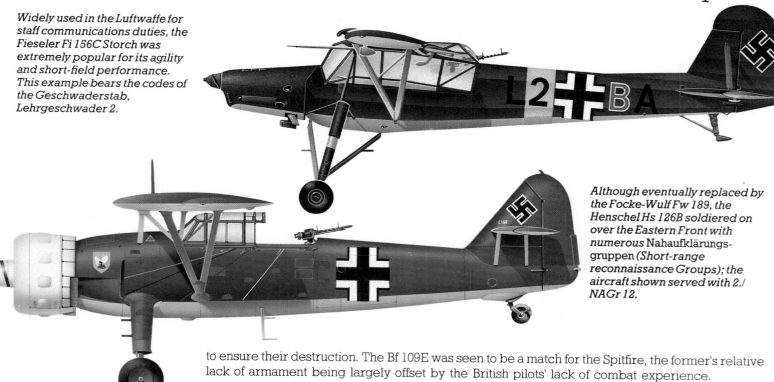

Widely used in the Luftwaffe for staff communications duties, the Fieseler Fi 156C Storch was extremely popular for its agility and short-field performance. This example bears the codes of the Geschwaderstab, Lehrgeschwader 2.

Although eventually replaced by the Focke-Wulf Fw 189, the Henschel Hs 126B soldiered on over the Eastern Front with numerous Nahaufklärungs-gruppen (Short-range reconnaissance Groups); the aircraft shown served with 2./NAGr 12.

to ensure their destruction. The Bf 109E was seen to be a match for the Spitfire, the former's relative lack of armament being largely offset by the British pilots' lack of combat experience.

First setback

The great Battle of Britain brought the greater part of the Luftwaffe into full-scale conflict with the British air defence system although, through lack of range in the Bf 109, the battle was largely confined to the south of England. The lessons of Dunkirk were that in daylight the formations of Do 17s, He 111s and Ju 87s required close escort and, in the light of the Bf 110's vulnerability (particularly in the presence of Hurricanes), this resulted in the Bf 109 being tied to the bomber formations as close escort; in so doing, the Luftwaffe was restricted twofold: the single-seat fighters could not meet the defending fighters on equal terms, and the bombers could not at least in safety and in daylight venture further than some 100 miles (160 km) beyond the English south and east coasts.

The Battle of Britain represented the first major setback for the Luftwaffe, both in matériel and morale. None of its aircraft, with the likely exception of the Bf 109, was seen to be invincible, least of all the vaunted Ju 87 and the Bf 110, the former having been withdrawn as being wholly unsuitable in the continuing presence of enemy fighters.

It was at this point, the first turning point of the war, that the Luftwaffe High Command (OKL) realized that considerable improvement of its aircraft was now needed, and quickly, if German initiative in the war was to be maintained, and it was in the autumn of 1940 that the German aircraft industry, hitherto operating at no more than walking pace, was ordered to gear itself for massive efforts to support the great assault on Russia which Hitler was already planning for 1941.

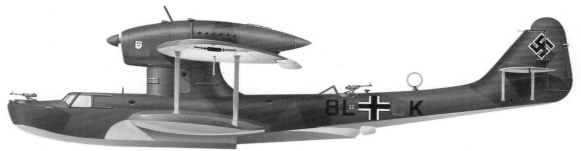

The Dornier Do 18D (here shown in the markings of 2. Staffel, Küstenfliegergruppe 906, based at Kamp/Pomerania during the winter of 1939-40) was developed from the pre-war transatlantic mail carrier and was employed on air-sea rescue and coastal reconnaissance duties.

The 'duck-in-clogs' insignia identifies this Blohm und Voss Bv 138C-1 (7R+RL) three-engine flying-boat as belonging to 3. Staffel, See-Aufklärungsgruppe 125 (Maritime Reconnaissance Group 125), based at Constanza, Romania for duties over the Black Sea in April 1943. A total of 279 Bv 138s was built between 1938 and 1943.

Typifying the style of Luftwaffe air support operations during the great German land advances of the first two years of the war, this scene depicts Ju 52/3m transports delivering fuel stocks for a Bf 110 unit.

Multi-front Nightmare

Complicated by Britain's dogged survival of the air assaults of 1940-1, Hitler's critical timetable for the conquest of Europe demanded a speedy victory over Russia, but simultaneous war on Western, Eastern and Southern fronts created an impossible strain on the Axis resources.

Among the bomber units switched from the night assault on Britain to the Eastern Front in 1941 was KG 55 'Greif' (Griffin Wing), one of whose Heinkel He 111Hs is seen here being armed prior to a raid.

As if reluctant to concede defeat in the daylight skies over the Britain in September 1940, Goering ordered the Luftwaffe to commence a prolonged night assault against British towns and cities, an offensive that was to last for almost nine months and of which the principal target was London, the vulnerable hub of British commerce and government that lay within easy reach of all German bombers with full bomb bays. Night after night the Heinkel He 111s, Dornier Do 17s and Junkers Ju 88s droned their way through darkened skies, scarcely troubled by the paltry British night-fighter defences.

Though the British civil population (and its morale) was the Luftwaffe's target, attempts were made to strike specific strategic objectives, often involving long flights over hostile territory. For

German Warplanes of World War II

The Heinkel He 111H was a rugged heavy bomber by early wartime standards, whose performance and load-carrying abilities were roughly comparable with those of the RAF's Wellington but, like the British aircraft, was transferred to the night bombing role after heavy losses sustained by day.

such purposes a new navigational tactic (the use of specialist pathfinding bombers) was brought into operation. It was the task of Kampfgruppe 100, equipped with special He 111s, to employ special radio aids (*X-Geräte*, receiving HF signals transmitted by a *Knickebein*, or a 'crooked leg', transmitter) to find and illuminate the target for the benefit of the main raiding force. In due course the British evolved means to distort the enemy signals and thereby prevent the concentration of an enemy raid; these countermeasures were the harbingers of a whole new science of radio and radar warfare that has flourished ever since.

By May 1941 Hitler's attack on Russia lay only a month away, and most of the *Kampfgeschwader* (bomber groups) were moved from France and Belgium to the East in readiness. It was at this time

Groundcrew prepare a Heinkel He 111H for flight; the nose insignia denotes KG 26 'Löwen-Geschwader' (Lion Wing), a bomber unit that was based at Stavanger, Norway, early in the Battle of Britain; it flew only one major daylight raid, on 15 August 1940, but suffered prohibitive losses.

After the Battle of Britain and the 'Blitz' of 1940-1 the Heinkel He 111 was moved to other war theatres and scarcely ever again appeared over Britain, although it continued to give sterling service in other roles right up to the end of the war.

that the first examples of a new bomber, the Dornier Do 217, were being delivered to units in France, at first to join the Focke-Wulf Fw 200 in anti-shipping duties over the Atlantic. The Do 217 was a much-improved and modernized development of the plainly obsolescent Do 17, being able to carry twice the bombload and capable of a speed of 320 mph (515 km/h). In time the Do 217 became one of the mainstays of the Luftwaffe's bomber force in the West.

Other developments had occurred during the winter of 1940-1. Italy had entered the war during the final death struggles of France in June 1940 and in due course embarked on a number of

Dornier Do 17

History and Notes
Designed to meet a commercial requirement for a high-speed mailplane issued in 1933, the attractive twin-engine Dornier Do 17 first appeared in prototype form with single fin and rudder, but the exceptionally slim fuselage resulted in the aircraft being abandoned on account of cramped accommodation. Rescued from oblivion, the prototypes were re-evaluated as high-speed bombers and, with twin fins and rudders, the Do 17 was ordered into production as the Do 17E and Do 17F, bomber and reconnaissance versions respectively, in 1936; both versions saw considerable service in the Spanish Civil war from 1937 onwards. Other prewar versions were the Do 17M bomber and the Do 17P reconnaissance aircraft, these being standard service aircraft with the Luftwaffe during 1939-40, the former with 900-hp (671-kW) Bramo radials and the latter with 865-hp (645-kW) BMW 132N radials.

The most important version was the Do 17Z which featured a deepened and extensively glazed nose, and some idea of the importance attached to this version by the Luftwaffe may be gained by the 352 aircraft on operational charge at the end of 1939. These four-seat bombers were produced in a number of versions, the Do 17 Z-1 having an armament of four 7.92-mm (0.31-in) guns and a bombload of 1,102 lb (500 kg), the Do 17 Z-2 having 1,000-hp (746-kW) Bramo engines and an armament of up to eight 7.92-mm (0.31-in) guns and a bombload of 2,205 lb (1000 kg), the Do 17Z-3 being photo-reconnaissance aircraft, the Do 17Z-4 being a dual-control trainer and the Do

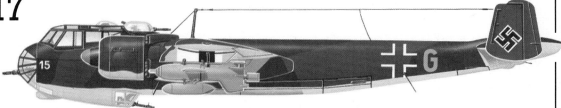

The Dornier Do 217 represented an ingenious update of the ageing Do 17; this Do 217E-5 was adapted to carry two Henschel Hs 293A stand-off guided weapons under the wings.

17Z-6 and Do 17Z-10 Kauz (Screech Owl) being night-fighters; the last, produced in 1940, featured a nose armament of two 20-mm and four 7.92-mm (0.31-in) guns.

Specification: Dornier Do 17Z-2
Origin: Germany
Type: four-crew medium bomber
Powerplant: two 1,000-hp (746-kW) Bramo 323P radial piston engines
Performance: maximum speed 255 mph (410 km/h) at 13,125 ft (4000 m); service ceiling 26,900 ft (8200 m); maximum range 845 miles (1360 km)

Weights: empty 11,486 lb (5210 kg); maximum take-off 18,937 lb (8590 kg)
Dimensions: span 59 ft 0⅝ (18.00 m); length 52 ft 9¾ in (16.10 m); height 14 ft 11¼ in (4.55 m); wing area 592.01 sq ft (55.00 m²)

Armament: bombload of up to 2,205 lb (1000 kg) and a variable defensive armament of up to eight 7.92-mm (0.31-in) MG 15 flexible guns disposed around crew cabin.

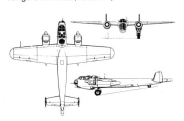

Dornier Do 217E-2

Light bombs stacked under a Dornier Do 17Z-2 of 10./KG 2 'Holzhammer' (Wooden Hammer Wing).

Heinkel He 111

History and Notes

Longest-serving medium bomber of the Luftwaffe, the Heinkel He 111 stemmed from a design by Siegfried and Walter Günter for a dual-purpose commercial transport/bomber produced in 1934 and flown on 24 February 1935. Early versions featured conventional stepped windscreen and elliptical wing leading edge, and a bomber version with these features (He 111B-1) served with the Legion Cóndor in the Spanish Civil War. The first production version with straight wing leading edge was the He 111F, and the He 111P incorporated a fully-glazed asymmetric nose without external windscreen step. He 111Ps with DB 601As engines were delivered to the Luftwaffe in 1939 before production switched to the most widely-used variant, the He 111H with Junkers Jumo 211 engines; sub-variant of this series formed the backbone of the Luftwaffe's bomber force between 1940 and 1943; they took part in numerous raids in the Battle of Britain and were flown by the pathfinder unit, KGr 100. The first version to carry torpedoes was the He 111H-6, followed by the He 111H-15; the He 111H-8 was fitted with a large and cumbersome balloon cable fender; the He 111H-11/R2 was a glider tug for the Go 242, while pathfinder versions with special radio were the He 111H-14 and He 111H-18; the He 111H-16 featured increased gun armament, and the He 111H-20 included 16-paratroop transport, night bomber and glider tug sub-variants. The He 111H-22 carried a single Fi 103 flying bomb and was used against the UK late in 1944. The most extraordinary of all was the He 111Z Zwilling (Twin) which consisted of two He 111Hs joined together with a new wing and fifth engine; it was used mainly to tow the huge Me 321 Gigant gliders. A total of about 7,300 He 111s was built.

Specification: Heinkel He 111H-16
Origin: Germany
Type: five-crew medium bomber
Powerplant: two 1,350-hp (1007-kW) Junkers Jumo 211F inline piston engines
Performance: maximum speed 271 mph (436 mph) at 19,685 ft (6000 m); climb to 19,685 ft (6000 m) in 42.0 minutes; service ceiling 21,980 ft (6700 m); range 1,212 miles (1950 km)
Weights: empty 19,136 lb (8680 kg); maximum take-off 30,865 lb (14000 kg)
Dimensions: span 74 ft 1¾ in (22.60 m); length 53 ft 9½ in (16.40 m); height 13 ft 1¼ in (3.40 m); wing area 931.07 sq ft (86.59 m²)
Armament: one 20-mm MG FF cannon in nose, one 13-mm (0.51-in) MG 131 gun in dorsal position, two 7.92-mm (0.31-in) MG 15 guns in rear of ventral gondola and two 7.92-mm (0.31-in) guns in each of two beam positions, plus a bombload of 4,409 lb (2000 kg) internally and 4,409 lb (200 kg) externally

A Heinkel He 111H flying over London's dockland during the early evening raid of 7 September 1940 – the raid that marked the end of the Luftwaffe's assault on RAF fighter bases, and incidentally represented Goering's fatal error which cost him likely victory in the Battle of Britain.

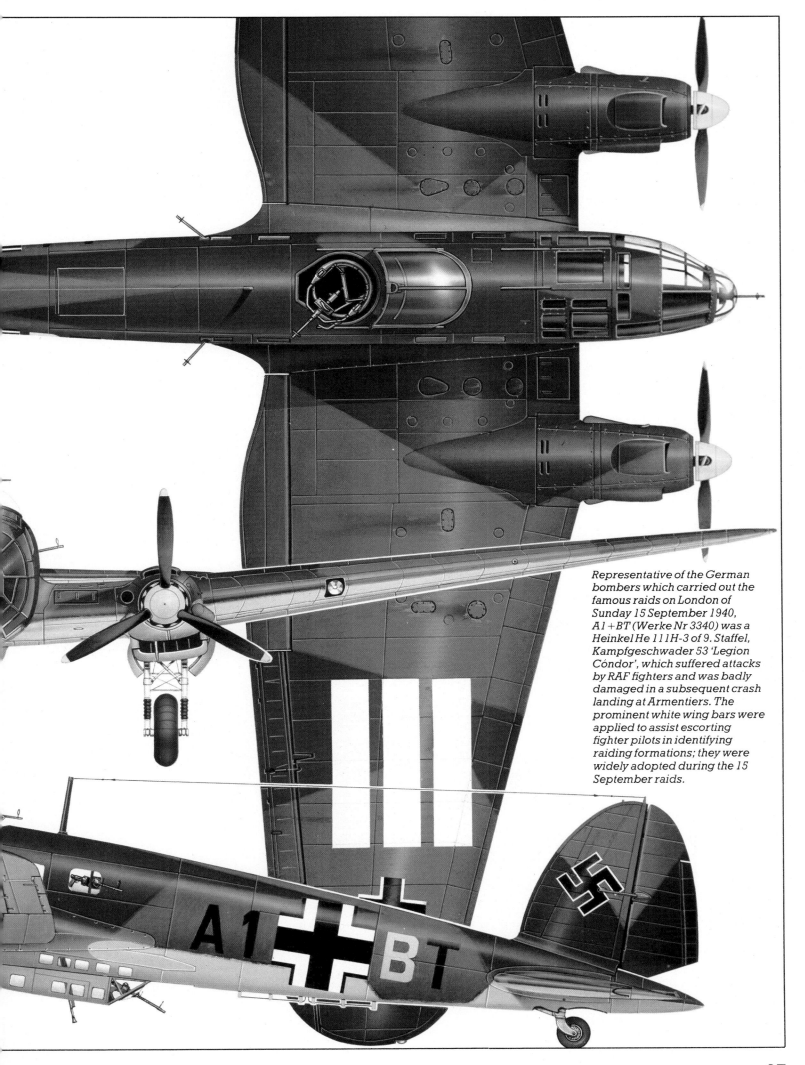

Representative of the German bombers which carried out the famous raids on London of Sunday 15 September 1940, A1+BT (Werke Nr 3340) was a Heinkel He 111H-3 of 9. Staffel, Kampfgeschwader 53 'Legion Cóndor', which suffered attacks by RAF fighters and was badly damaged in a subsequent crash landing at Armentiers. The prominent white wing bars were applied to assist escorting fighter pilots in identifying raiding formations; they were widely adopted during the 15 September raids.

German Warplanes of World War II

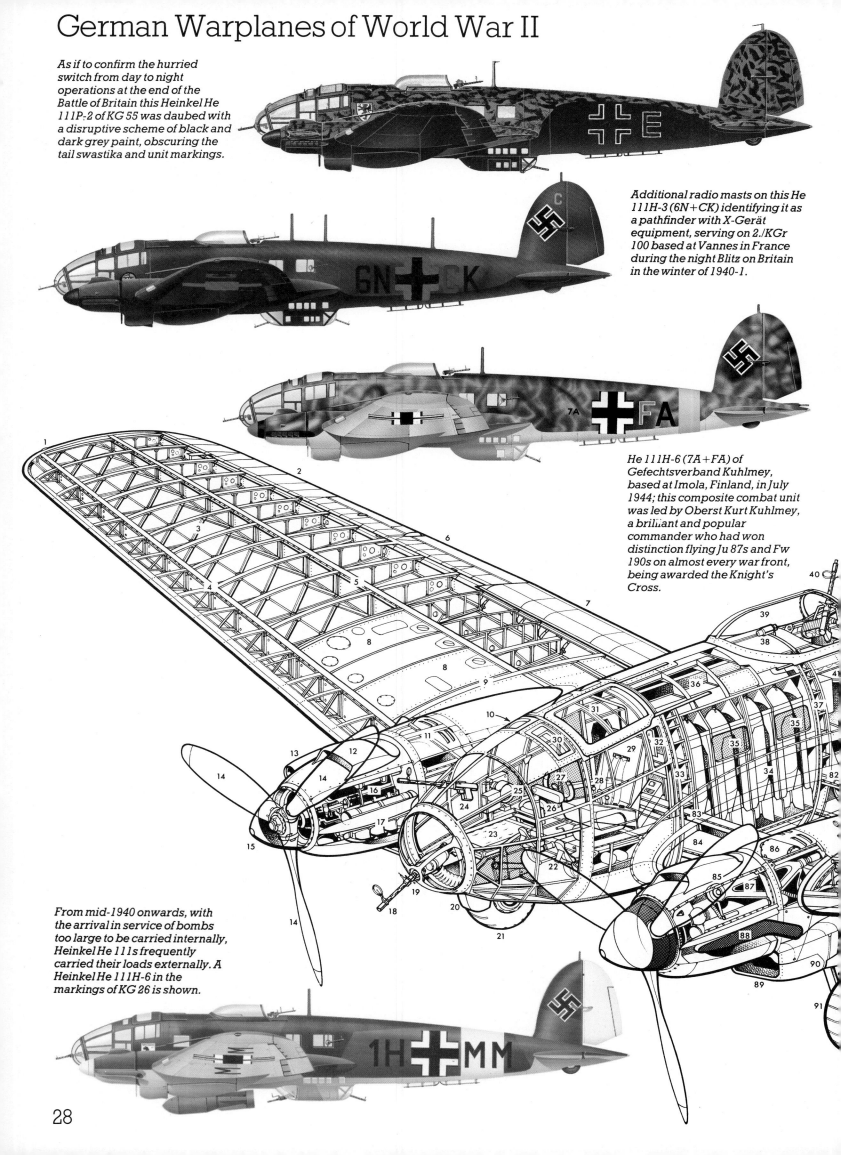

As if to confirm the hurried switch from day to night operations at the end of the Battle of Britain this Heinkel He 111P-2 of KG 55 was daubed with a disruptive scheme of black and dark grey paint, obscuring the tail swastika and unit markings.

Additional radio masts on this He 111H-3 (6N+CK) identifying it as a pathfinder with X-Gerät equipment, serving on 2./KGr 100 based at Vannes in France during the night Blitz on Britain in the winter of 1940-1.

He 111H-6 (7A+FA) of Gefechtsverband Kuhlmey, based at Imola, Finland, in July 1944; this composite combat unit was led by Oberst Kurt Kuhlmey, a brilliant and popular commander who had won distinction flying Ju 87s and Fw 190s on almost every war front, being awarded the Knight's Cross.

From mid-1940 onwards, with the arrival in service of bombs too large to be carried internally, Heinkel He 111s frequently carried their loads externally. A Heinkel He 111H-6 in the markings of KG 26 is shown.

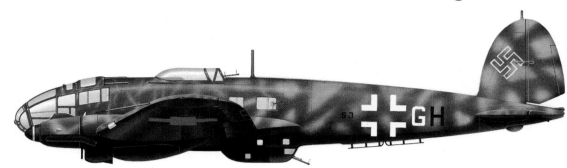

During the final days of the Third Reich Heinkel He 111s were employed to drop supplies to isolated German forces. This He 111H-20 (5J+GH) belonged to I/KG-4 'General Wever' based at Dresden-Klotzsche in April 1945.

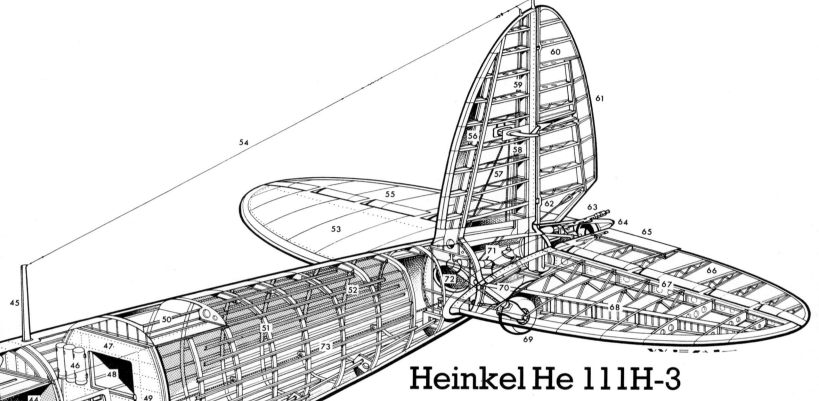

Heinkel He 111H-3

© Pilot Press Limited

1 Starboard navigation light
2 Starboard aileron
3 Wing ribs
4 Forward spar
5 Rear spar
6 Aileron tab
7 Starboard flap
8 Fuel tank access panel
9 Wing centre section/outer panel break line
10 Inboard fuel tank (154 Imp gal/700 litre capacity) position between nacelle and fuselage
11 Oil tank cooling louvres
12 Oil cooler air intake
13 Supercharger air intake
14 Three-blade VDM airscrew

15 Airscrew pitch-change mechanism
16 Junkers Jumo 211 D-1 12-cylinder inverted-vee liquid-cooled engine
17 Exhaust manifold
18 Nose-mounted 7.9-mm MG 15 machine-gun
19 Ikaria ball-and-socket gun mounting (offset to starboard)
20 Bomb sight housing (offset to starboard)
21 Starboard mainwheel
22 Rudder pedals
23 Bomb aimer's horizontal pad
24 Additional 7.9-mm MG 15 machine-gun (fitted by forward maintenance units)

25 Repeater compass
26 Bomb aimer's folding seat
27 Control column
28 Throttles
29 Pilot's seat
30 Retractable auxiliary windscreen (for use when pilot's seat in elevated position)
31 Sliding entry panel
32 Forward fuselage bulkhead
33 Double-frame station
34 Port ESAC bomb bay (vertical stowage)
35 Fuselage windows (blanked)
36 Central gangway between bomb bays
37 Double-frame station
38 Direction finder

39 Dorsal gunner's (forward) sliding canopy
40 Dorsal 7.9-mm MG 15 machine-gun
41 Dorsal gunner's cradle seat
42 FuG 10 radio equipment
43 Fuselage window
44 Armoured bulkhead (8-mm)
45 Aerial mast
46 bomb flares
47 Unarmoured bulkhead
48 Rear fuselage access cut-out
49 Port 7.9-mm beam MG 15 machine-gun

50 Dinghy stowage
51 Fuselage frames
52 Stringers
53 Starboard tailplane
54 Aerial
55 Starboard elevator
56 Tailfin forward spar
57 Tailfin structure
58 Rudder balance
59 Tailfin rear spar/rudder post
60 Rudder construction
61 Rudder tab
62 Tab actuator (starboard surface)
63 Remotely-controlled 7.9-mm MG 17 machine-gun in

tail cone (fitted to some aircraft only)
64 Rear navigation light
65 Elevator tab
66 Elevator structure
67 Elevator hinge line
68 Tailplane front spar
69 Semi-retractable tailwheel
70 Tailwheel shock-absorber
71 Tail surface control linkage
72 Fuselage/tailfin frame
73 Control pulley
74 Push-pull control rods
75 Observation window pad
76 Observation window fairing

77 Glazed observation window in floor
78 Ventral aft-firing 7.9-mm MG 15 machine-gun in tail of 'Sterbebett' ('Death-bed') bath
79 Ventral bath entry hatch
80 Ventral gunner's horizontal pad
81 Forward-firing 20-mm (Oerlikon) MG FF cannon (for anti-shipping operations)
82 Rear spar carry-through
83 Forward spar carry-through
84 Oil cooler

85 Anti-vibration engine mount
86 Oil tank
87 Engine bearer
88 Exhaust flame-damper shroud
89 Radiator air intake
90 Radiator bath
91 Port mainwheel
92 Mainwheel leg
93 Retraction mechanism
94 Mainwheel door (outer)
95 Multi-screw wing attachment
96 Trailing-aerial tube (to starboard of ventral bath)

97 Rear spar attachment
98 Port outboard fuel tank (220 Imp gal/1000 litre capacity)
99 Flap control rod
100 Landing light
101 Pitot head
102 Pitot head heater/wing leading-edge de-icer
103 Flap and aileron coupling
104 Flap structure
105 Aileron tab
106 Tab actuator
107 Rear spar
108 Forward spar
109 Port aileron
110 Port navigation light

German Warplanes of World War II

adventures in Egypt and East Africa, supplementing the dire course of events already taking place in the Balkans. These adventures rapidly became bogged down as a result of inadequate planning and unexpectedly stubborn Allied resistance, so calls for assistance had brought a growing force of Luftwaffe aircraft to the Mediterranean, and in due course to the Balkans.

A Dornier Do 17Z, probably of KG 2 serving in the Balkans in 1941; at that time the Do 17 was regarded as obsolescent and was slowly being replaced by He 111s and Ju 88s.

Further expansions

As the first *Gruppe* of specially tropicalized Messerschmitt Bf 109Es (I Gruppe of JG 27) arrived early in 1941 in Sicily to support what was later to become famous as General Rommel's Deutsches Afrika Korps, Hitler determined to eliminate Yugoslavia and Greece as a potential threat to his southern flank of the future Russian front (and thereby extricate Italy from an embarrassing

Showing to excellent effect the Luftwaffe's desert camouflage, this Messerschmitt Bf 109E-4/ Trop served with I/JG 27 under Hauptmann Eduard Neumann during 1941 in North Africa.

A Junkers Ju 88A-1 (9K+GL) of I/KG 51 'Edelweiss' based at Melun-Villaroche, France, October 1940. The black undersides and toned-down markings were adopted during the night Blitz on Britain of the winter 1940-1.

Junkers Ju 88A-4 (4D+DT) of 9./ KG 30 'Adler Geschwader' (Eagle Wing). This Geschwader's III Gruppe was particularly successful in its attacks on Allied shipping in the Mediterranean during 1941, as illustrated by the tally painted on this Ju 88's fin.

stalemate). British and Greek Hawker Hurricanes and Gloster Gladiators, which had successfully matched the Italian aircraft, now faced the modern German air force. Within six weeks the German army and the Luftwaffe were once more triumphant, and the British were forced to evacuate their forces, first to Crete and finally to Egypt. The Junkers Ju 88s in particular left their mark on the Greek campaign, carrying out a number of brilliant low-level raids on ports and airfields. In the subsequent invasion of Crete the Luftwaffe once more employed airborne forces, dropping large numbers of paratroops from and landing others in Junkers Ju 52/ms, and flying in small groups of troops in DFS 230 gliders, though sustaining very heavy losses in the process. (Already there were German plans to produce a true assault glider, the Gotha Go 242, but having only been initiated less than a year before these were not ready in time for the Crete operation.)

Thus by mid-1941 the nature of the war had been decided for Germany as one involving that traditional nightmare, enemies to the east and west (and now to the south), and in the air. Only Turkey, Switzerland, Sweden, Spain and Portugal remained neutral; Italy, Austria, Hungary, Romania, Bulgaria and Finland had or were about to join the Axis, while Poland, Czechoslovakia, Denmark, Norway, the Netherlands, Belgium, France, Yugoslavia, Albania and Greece had all been subjugated by Germany or Italy. In due course German aircraft were built in many of these countries to supplement production in the 'Fatherland'.

It is worthwhile at this point, on the eve of Hitler's assault on the Soviet Union, to take stock of the

The Ju 88 was one of the most adaptable of all German aircraft of the war and served on almost every front from the north of Norway to the Mediterranean, and from the night Blitz on Britain to the assault on the Soviet Union.

German Warplanes of World War II

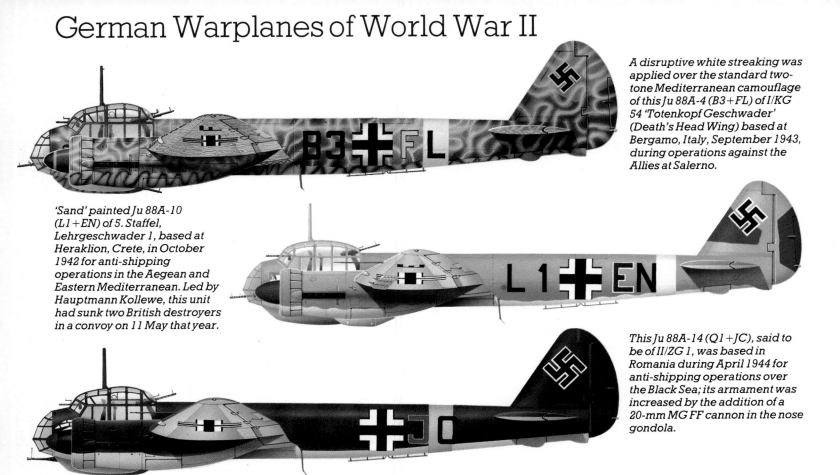

A disruptive white streaking was applied over the standard two-tone Mediterranean camouflage of this Ju 88A-4 (B3+FL) of I/KG 54 'Totenkopf Geschwader' (Death's Head Wing) based at Bergamo, Italy, September 1943, during operations against the Allies at Salerno.

'Sand' painted Ju 88A-10 (L1+EN) of 5. Staffel, Lehrgeschwader 1, based at Heraklion, Crete, in October 1942 for anti-shipping operations in the Aegean and Eastern Mediterranean. Led by Hauptmann Kollewe, this unit had sunk two British destroyers in a convoy on 11 May that year.

This Ju 88A-14 (Q1+JC), said to be of II/ZG 1, was based in Romania during April 1944 for anti-shipping operations over the Black Sea; its armament was increased by the addition of a 20-mm MG FF cannon in the nose gondola.

Luftwaffe and its equipment. Most important arrival in service at this time was the new Messerschmitt Bf 109F, a considerably cleaned-up development of the now-ageing Bf 109E and powered by the beefy Daimler-Benz DB 601N or E. Its top speed of 391 mph (630 km/h) gave it a substantial edge over the early Supermarine Spitfires and Hurricanes of the RAF and over anything yet being flown by the Russians.

Eastern Front

The bomber force in the East was composed almost entirely of He 111s and Ju 88s, the former equipping three *Geschwader* (with about 320 aircraft), soon to be joined by four further *Gruppen* (another 120 aircraft), and the latter two *Geschwader* (with some 200 aircraft). Junkers Ju 87s, once more brought into action in support of the *Blitzkrieg,* equipped seven *Stukagruppen* with around 270 aircraft, including a number of Ju 87Rs with long-range tanks.

Elsewhere the German air force was pared to the bone to allow the assembly of the greatest possible concentration of air power in the East. In France fighter defences were reduced to two *Geschwader* (JG 2 and JG 26) of Bf 109Fs but, reflecting the growing importance of operations over

Two Messerschmitt Bf 109Fs of III/JG 54 'Grünherz' (Green Hearts) serving on the Leningrad front during the autumn of 1941. Commanded by Major Hannes Trautloft, this Geschwader had already achieved its 1,000th air combat victory in August that year.

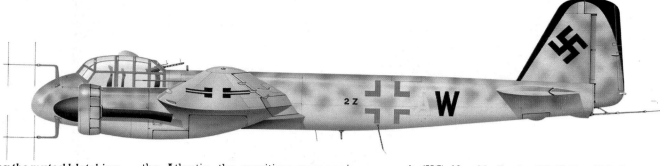

Illustrating the muted blotching of Luftwaffe night fighters during the late war period, this Ju 88G-7a (2Z+AW) of IV/NJG 6, winter 1944-5, has had its vertical tail painted to represent that of the earlier Ju 88C night fighter.

the Atlantic, the maritime reconnaissance unit (KG 40 with Focke-Wulf Fw 200 Condors) was strengthened by the arrival of the first more heavily-armed Fw 200Cs. In Norway, and also deployed for anti-shipping attacks, there remained two *Gruppen* of He 111s (I and III/KG 26), and a *Geschwader* of Ju 88s. In the Mediterranean theatre an autonomous *Fliegerkorps* (Air Corps) deployed two *Gruppen* of tropicalized Bf 109Es (soon replaced by Bf 109Fs) and one of Ju 87s. In the Balkans air defence rested upon one *Gruppe* of Bf 109s, though theoretically this was available to cover the south Russian front.

From the outset of Operation 'Barbarossa' (the attack on Russia) the Luftwaffe seized and retained total air supremacy over the front. On the first day the Russian conceded the loss of over 1,200 aircraft, the majority destroyed on the ground by surprise attack. The *Jagdverband* chopped up all air opposition and very soon many Bf 109 pilots were amassing personal air victory tallies far in excess of any score ever before achieved. After an initial phase of devastating attacks on Soviet airfields, a series of heavy raids on Moscow was carried out by an average of more than 100 Ju 88s and He 111s. In the north, Ju 87s attacked the Soviet fleet at Kronshtadt, sinking the battleship *Marat*. (The pilot involved in this success was one Hans-Ulrich Rudel, by far the most successful dive-bomber pilot of the war.)

Night defence

Although the war situation in mid-1941 was fairly satisfactory for Germany, with the initiative on almost all fronts still firmly in her grasp, the steady build-up of British strength was giving concern, especially in the slow but steady increase of RAF bomber strength in the West. Daylight attacks on France and the Low Countries were as yet pinpricks, but the growing weight of night attacks on the German homeland had forced Goering to sanction the rapid build-up of night-fighter forces. This could be achieved largely by adaptation of existing fighters, in particular the Messerschmitt Bf 110 (which had not exactly excelled in daylight) and the Ju 88C (itself a *Zerstörer* adaptation of the bomber version).

As in the RAF, little serious attention had been given to the night-fighter by the Luftwaffe before

Lichtenstein radar-equipped Messerschmitt Bf 110G of a Luftwaffe night fighter unit. These aircraft constitued the major part of Germany's night air defences and took a very heavy toll of RAF Lancasters and Halifaxes during the last two years of the war.

Junkers Ju 88

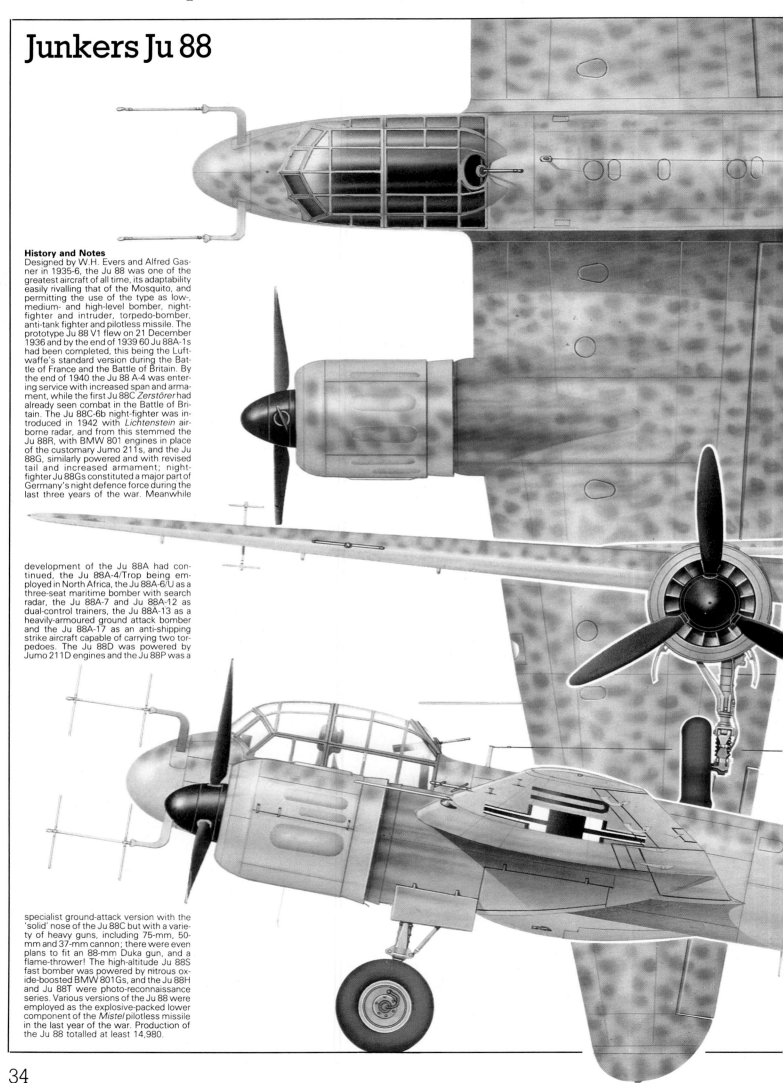

History and Notes

Designed by W.H. Evers and Alfred Gasner in 1935-6, the Ju 88 was one of the greatest aircraft of all time, its adaptability easily rivalling that of the Mosquito, and permitting the use of the type as low-, medium- and high-level bomber, night-fighter and intruder, torpedo-bomber, anti-tank fighter and pilotless missile. The prototype Ju 88 V1 flew on 21 December 1936 and by the end of 1939 60 Ju 88A-1s had been completed, this being the Luftwaffe's standard version during the Battle of France and the Battle of Britain. By the end of 1940 the Ju 88 A-4 was entering service with increased span and armament, while the first Ju 88C *Zerstörer* had already seen combat in the Battle of Britain. The Ju 88C-6b night-fighter was introduced in 1942 with *Lichtenstein* airborne radar, and from this stemmed the Ju 88R, with BMW 801 engines in place of the customary Jumo 211s, and the Ju 88G, similarly powered and with revised tail and increased armament; night-fighter Ju 88Gs constituted a major part of Germany's night defence force during the last three years of the war. Meanwhile development of the Ju 88A had continued, the Ju 88A-4/Trop being employed in North Africa, the Ju 88A-6/U as a three-seat maritime bomber with search radar, the Ju 88A-7 and Ju 88A-12 as dual-control trainers, the Ju 88A-13 as a heavily-armoured ground attack bomber and the Ju 88A-17 as an anti-shipping strike aircraft capable of carrying two torpedoes. The Ju 88D was powered by Jumo 211D engines and the Ju 88P was a specialist ground-attack version with the 'solid' nose of the Ju 88C but with a variety of heavy guns, including 75-mm, 50-mm and 37-mm cannon; there were even plans to fit an 88-mm Duka gun, and a flame-thrower! The high-altitude Ju 88S fast bomber was powered by nitrous oxide-boosted BMW 801Gs, and the Ju 88H and Ju 88T were photo-reconnaissance series. Various versions of the Ju 88 were employed as the explosive-packed lower component of the *Mistel* pilotless missile in the last year of the war. Production of the Ju 88 totalled at least 14,980.

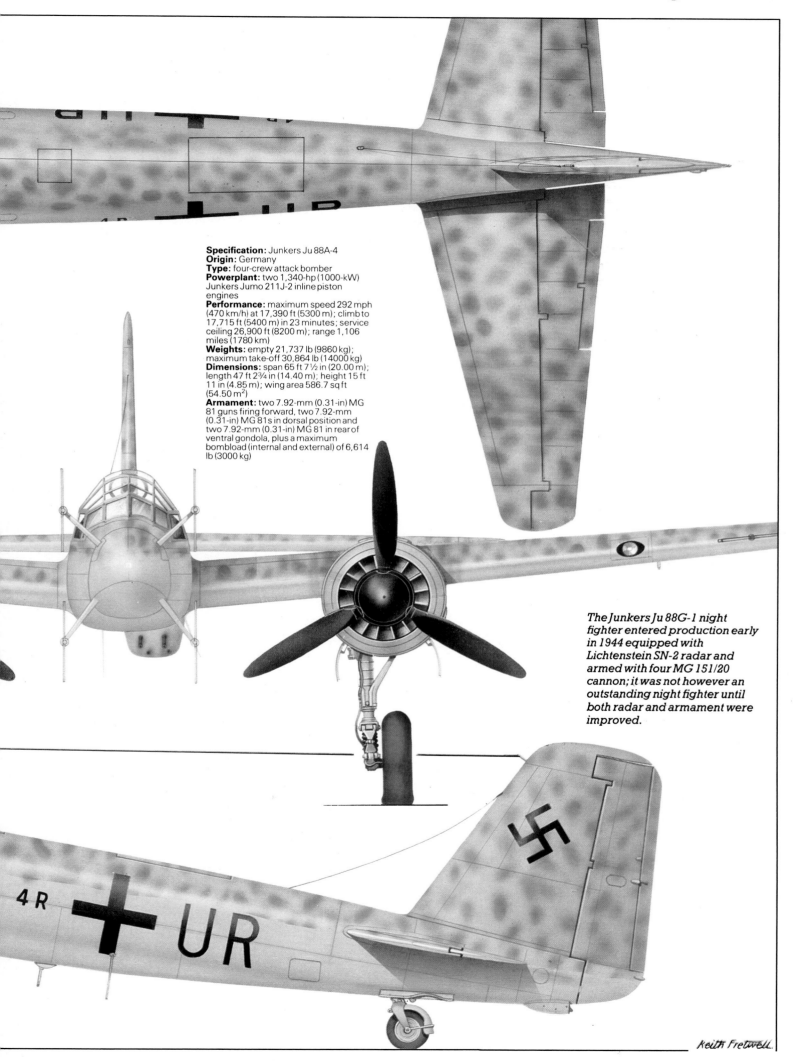

Specification: Junkers Ju 88A-4
Origin: Germany
Type: four-crew attack bomber
Powerplant: two 1,340-hp (1000-kW) Junkers Jumo 211J-2 inline piston engines
Performance: maximum speed 292 mph (470 km/h) at 17,390 ft (5300 m); climb to 17,715 ft (5400 m) in 23 minutes; service ceiling 26,900 ft (8200 m); range 1,106 miles (1780 km)
Weights: empty 21,737 lb (9860 kg); maximum take-off 30,864 lb (14000 kg)
Dimensions: span 65 ft 7½ in (20.00 m); length 47 ft 2¾ in (14.40 m); height 15 ft 11 in (4.85 m); wing area 586.7 sq ft (54.50 m²)
Armament: two 7.92-mm (0.31-in) MG 81 guns firing forward, two 7.92-mm (0.31-in) MG 81s in dorsal position and two 7.92-mm (0.31-in) MG 81 in rear of ventral gondola, plus a maximum bombload (internal and external) of 6,614 lb (3000 kg)

The Junkers Ju 88G-1 night fighter entered production early in 1944 equipped with Lichtenstein SN-2 radar and armed with four MG 151/20 cannon; it was not however an outstanding night fighter until both radar and armament were improved.

Keith Fretwell

A Junkers Ju 88A-4 of III Gruppe, Lehrgeschwader 1 on the Eastern Front in 1942, seen here carrying a 551-lb (250-kg) and a 1,102-lb (500-kg) bomb.

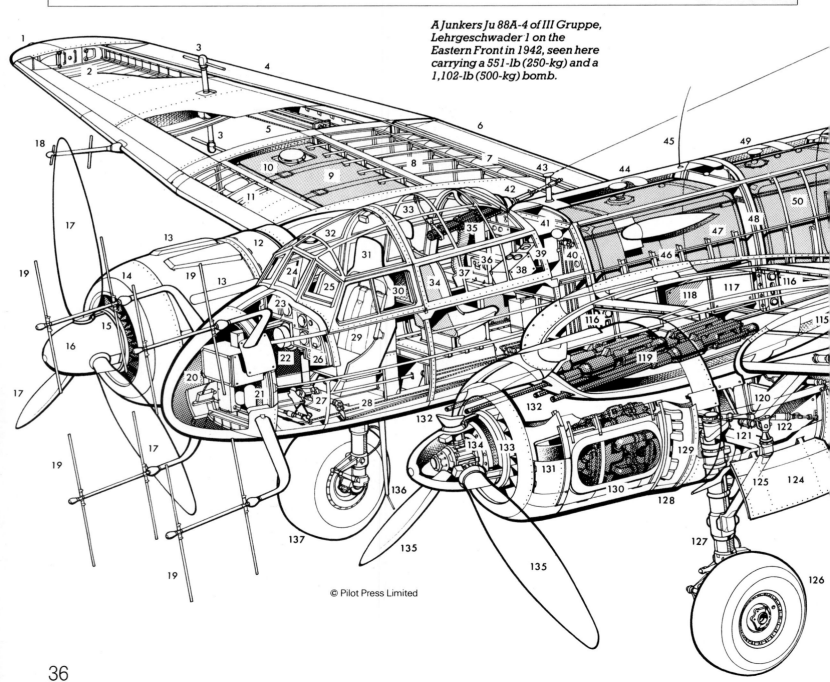

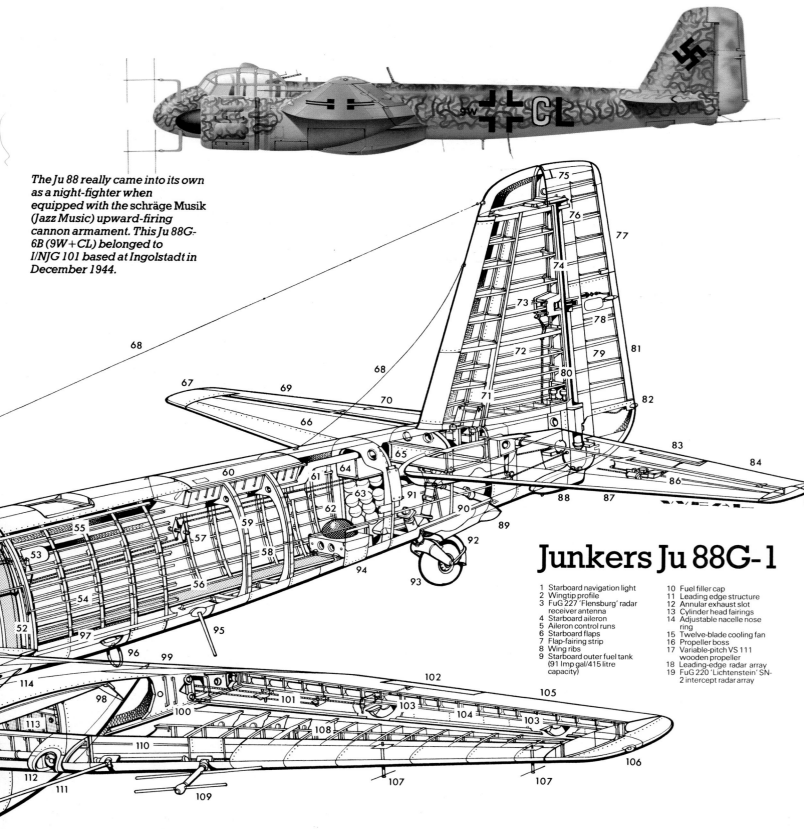

The Ju 88 really came into its own as a night-fighter when equipped with the schräge Musik (Jazz Music) upward-firing cannon armament. This Ju 88G-6B (9W+CL) belonged to I/NJG 101 based at Ingolstadt in December 1944.

Junkers Ju 88G-1

1 Starboard navigation light
2 Wingtip profile
3 FuG 227 'Flensburg' radar receiver antenna
4 Starboard aileron
5 Aileron control runs
6 Starboard flaps
7 Flap-fairing strip
8 Wing ribs
9 Starboard outer fuel tank (91 Imp gal/415 litre capacity)
10 Fuel filler cap
11 Leading edge structure
12 Annular exhaust slot
13 Cylinder head fairings
14 Adjustable nacelle nose ring
15 Twelve-blade cooling fan
16 Propeller boss
17 Variable-pitch VS 111 wooden propeller
18 Leading-edge radar array
19 FuG 220 'Lichtenstein' SN-2 intercept radar array

20 Nose cone
21 Forward armoured bulkhead
22 Gyro compass
23 Instrument panel
24 Armour-glass windscreen
25 Folding seat
26 Control column
27 Rudder pedal/brake cylinder
28 Control runs
29 Pilot's armoured seat
30 Sliding window section
31 Headrest
32 Jettisonable canopy roof section
33 Gun restraint
34 Wireless operator/gunner's seat
35 Rheinmetall Borsig MG 131 machine-gun (13-mm calibre)
36 Radio equipment (FuG 10P HF, FuG 16ZY VHF, FuG 25 IFF)
37 Ammunition box (500 rounds of 13-mm)

38 FuG 220 'Lichtenstein' SN-2 indicator box
39 FuG 227 'Flensburg' indicator box
40 Control linkage
41 Bulkhead
42 Armoured gun mount
43 Aerial post traverse check
44 Fuel filler cap
45 Whip aerial
46 Forward fuselage fuel tank (105 Imp gal/480 litre capacity)
47 Fuselage horizontal construction joint
48 Bulkhead
49 Fuel filler cap
50 Aft fuselage fuel tank (230 Imp gal/1045 litre capacity)
51 Access hatch
52 Bulkhead
53 Control linkage access plate
54 Fuselage stringers
55 Upper longeron
56 Maintenance walkway
57 Control linkage

58 Horizontal construction joint
59 Z-section fuselage frames
60 Dinghy stowage
61 Fuel vent pipe
62 Master compass
63 Spherical oxygen bottles
64 Accumulator
65 Tailplane centre section carry-through
66 Starboard tailplane
67 Elevator balance
68 Aerial
69 Starboard elevator
70 Elevator tab
71 Tailfin forward spar/fuselage attachment
72 Tailfin structure
73 Rudder actuator
74 Rudder post
75 Rudder mass balance
76 Rudder upper hinge
77 Tailfin aft spar/fuselage attachment
78 Inspection/maintenance handhold
79 Rudder structure

80 Tailfin aft spar/fuselage attachment
81 Rudder tab (lower section)
82 Rear navigation light
83 Elevator tab
84 Port elevator
85 Elevator balance
86 Elevator tab actuator
87 Heated leading edge
88 Tail bumper/fuel vent outlet
89 Tailwheel doors
90 Tailwheel retraction mechanism
91 Shock absorber leg
92 Mudguard
93 Tailwheel
94 Access hatch
95 Fixed antenna
96 D/F loop
97 Lower longeron
98 Nacelle/flap fairing
99 Port flap
100 Wing centre/outer section attachment point
101 Aileron controls
102 Aileron tab (port only)

103 Aileron hinges
104 Rear spar
105 Port aileron
106 Port navigation light
107 FuG 101a radio altimeter antenna
108 Wing structure
109 Leading-edge radar array
110 Forward spar
111 Pitot head
112 Landing lamp
113 Mainwheel well rear bulkhead
114 Port outer fuel tank location (91 Imp gal/415 litre capacity)
115 Ventral gun pack (offset to port)
116 Ball-and-socket fuselage/wing attachment points
117 Port inner fuel tank location (93.4 Imp gal/425 litre capacity)
118 Ammunition boxes for MG 151 cannon (200 rpg)
119 Mauser MG 151/20 cannon (four) of 20-mm calibre

120 Mainwheel leg retraction yoke
121 Leg pivot member
122 Mainwheel door actuating jack
123 Mainwheel door (rear section)
124 Mainwheel door (forward section)
125 Leg support strut
126 Port mainwheel
127 Mainwheel leg
128 Annular exhaust slot
129 Exhaust stubs (internal)
130 BMW 801D air-cooled radial engine (partly omitted for clarity)
131 Annular oil tank
132 Cannon muzzles (depressed five degrees)
133 Twelve-blade cooling fan
134 Propeller mechanism
135 Variable-pitch wooden VS 111 propeller
136 FuG 16ZY antenna
137 Starboard mainwheel

Henschel Hs 129

History and Notes

The single-seat ground-support Henschel Hs 129 was the outcome of an imaginative though somewhat speculative requirement issued by the German air ministry in 1937 for a heavily armoured twin-engine aircraft to perform an anti-tank role. Designed by Friedrich Nicolaus, the Hs 129 V1 prototype was first flown in 1938 with two 465-hp (347-kW) Argus As 410 inline engines; it proved to be underpowered, cramped for the pilot and sluggish on the controls. These severe criticisms resulted in re-engining some of the pre-production Hs 129A-0s with captured French 700-hp (522-kW) Gnome-Rhône 14M radials.

Development Hs 129B-0s, with these engines, increased cockpit space and electrically-operated trim tabs, were delivered in December 1941, followed by production Hs 129B-1s in 1942. The majority of Hs 129s served with units on the Eastern Front, playing an outstanding part in destroying Russian armour in the great battle of Kursk of July 1943, but also in North Africa where they met with less success. A large number of armament variations were developed, including the Hs 129B-1/R2 with a 30-mm MK 101 cannon under the nose with 30 rounds, the Hs 129B-3 with a 75-mm BK 7.5 anti-tank gun with 12 rounds, and numerous *Rüstsatz* variations combining light anti-personnel and fragmentation bombs with 7.92-mm (0.31-in), 13-mm (0.51-in), 15-mm (0.59-in), 20-mm and 30-mm guns. A total of 858 Hs 129s was built between 1942 and 1944 and, provided they were not opposed by defending fighters, their pilots did considerable damage amongst Russian armoured vehicles in the East, the 75-mm gun proving capable of penetrating the front armour of KV-1 and T-34 tanks.

A Henschel Hs 129B-2/R2 of IV(Pz)/SG 9, Czernowitz, March 1944. Commanded by the brilliant Major Bruno Meyer, this new unit operated on a roving commission over the Eastern Front in 1944.

Specification: Henschel Hs 129B-1/R2
Origin: Germany
Type: single-seat anti-tank ground-support aircraft
Powerplant: two 700-hp (522-kW) Gnome-Rhône 14M radial piston engines
Performance: maximum speed 253 mph (407 km/h) at 12,750 ft (3830 m); time to 9,845 ft (3000 m) in 7.0 minutes; service ceiling 29,530 ft (9000 m); range 348 miles (560 km)
Weights: empty 8,783 lb (3984 kg); maximum take-off 11,263 lb (5109 kg)

Armament: two 20-mm MG 151/20 and two 7.92-mm (0.31-in) MG 17 guns in nose, and one 30-mm MK 101 cannon with 30 rounds in fairing under the nose, plus a bombload of up to 772 lb (350 kg)

Dimensions: span 46 ft 7 in (14.20 m); length 31 ft 11¾ in (9.75 m); height 10 ft 8 in (3.25 m); wing area 312.16 sq ft (29.00 m²)

Henschel Hs 129B-1/R4

The Henschel Hs 129B eventually proved a fairly effective ground attack aircraft, though somewhat underpowered.

the war. When, in 1940, British (and French) bombers carried out a number of desultory night raids, darkness itself seemed to be the best defence as many bombers simply failed to find their targets. It was, however, the early raids on Berlin, the Ruhr and Italy (the last involving long trips over German-held territory) that speeded the formation of the first *Nachtjagdgeschwader* (night-fighter wings) and these were equipped with about 90 Bf 110Cs without specialized equipment. By June 1941, when three *Geschwader* (NJG 1, 2 and 3) had been formed, the Bf 110D, Bf 110F-4 and Bf 110G-4 had been or were being specially developed for night-fighting, as well as small numbers of Do 17s, Do 217s and Ju 88Cs. Only rudimentary radar was as yet being carried by the fighters, dependence being placed mainly upon Generalmajor Josef Kammhuber's *Himmelbett* system of ground radar which guided the night-fighter right up to its target; not surprisingly, early night victories were scarce.

1941 was a period of intense activity for the German aircraft industry as the earlier requirements bore fruit in the shape of numerous prototypes. In the ground-support role there was the radical twin-engine Henschel Hs 129, which had in fact first flown in 1939 but had been found to be ridiculously underpowered until re-engined with French Gnome-Rhône radials in 1941; now seen to be worth developing, it was ordered into production as the Hs 129B and joined the Luftwaffe in 1942.

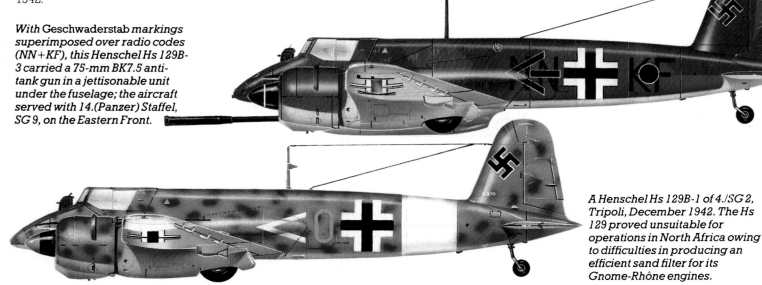

With Geschwaderstab *markings superimposed over radio codes (NN+KF), this Henschel Hs 129B-3 carried a 75-mm BK7.5 anti-tank gun in a jettisonable unit under the fuselage; the aircraft served with 14.(Panzer) Staffel, SG 9, on the Eastern Front.*

A Henschel Hs 129B-1 of 4./SG 2, Tripoli, December 1942. The Hs 129 proved unsuitable for operations in North Africa owing to difficulties in producing an efficient sand filter for its Gnome-Rhône engines.

A Heinkel He 177A-5 (V4+KN) of II Gruppe, Kampfgeschwader 1 'Hindenburg' based at Prowenhren, East Prussia, mid-1944. Led by Oberstleutnant Horst von Riesen, KG 1 assembled about 90 of these bombers for attacks on Russian communications and military concentrations.

A Heinkel He 177A-0 pre-production aircraft. These big bombers, originally intended to provide the Luftwaffe with a strategic bombing force, encountered so many development problems that they only entered service in any numbers during the last 18 months of the war.

Contender for the title of the war's most grotesque aircraft, the Blohm und Voss Bv 141 reconnaissance aircraft suffered endless difficulties and was abandoned in 1942 before entering production; the aircraft shown here (NC+RF) was the twelfth prototype, the Bv 141B-04.

The big four-engine Heinkel He 177 heavy bomber, whose engines were 'coupled' in two nacelles, had first flown in November 1939 but immediately ran into problems with engine overheating and tail flutter, and it was not until August 1941 that the first aircraft were delivered to KG 40 for service trials. Even then Luftwaffe crews complained bitterly about their aircraft, so that further development was required before the He 177A finally carried out its first raids in mid-1942.

The extraordinary Blohm und Voss Bv 141 was a single-engine short-range reconnaissance aircraft with a conventional fuselage but with the two-seat crew nacelle offset to starboard and with no starboard tailplane. The purpose of this unusual layout was to afford the crew increased field of vision and, although trials continued during the first three years of the war with more than a dozen prototypes, the Bv 141 was finally abandoned owing to the fact that the less-unorthodox Focke-Wulf Fw 189 was performing the task quite efficiently.

German Warplanes of World War II

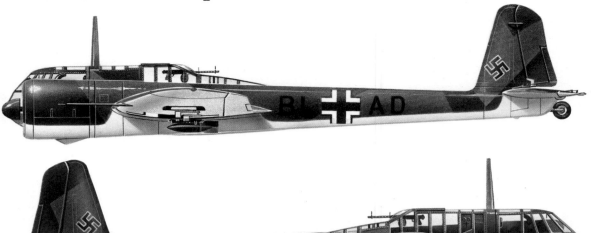

Characterized by the tall angular fin and rudder, the Blohm und Voss Bv 141A-0 (A-04 shown here) underwent trials at Rechlin in 1940 but was dropped in favour of the Focke-Wulf Fw 189 Uhu. Two years later plans were abandoned to form a special unit, Sonderstaffel 141, on the Eastern Front.

The Fw 189 Uhu (Owl) was a twin-boom twin-engine monoplane with central three/four-seat nacelle. It had flown as long ago as July 1938 (with its designer, Kurt Tank, at the controls), but it was not until 1942 that significant numbers of Fw 189A-1s and Fw 189A-2s started joining Aufklärungs-gruppe 10 'Tannenburg' and AufklGr 11 on the Eastern Front, finally replacing the venerable Hs 126.

Messerschmitt failure, Focke-Wulf success

Another aircraft that was doomed to eclipse at this time was the Messerschmitt Me 210, a *Zerstörer* that had been conceived in 1937, just as the Bf 110 was joining the Luftwaffe. Great hopes were attached to the Me 210 two-seat twin-engine fighter and a special unit, Erprobungsgruppe 210, was formed early in the summer of 1940 to introduce the aircraft into Luftwaffe service. In the event the Me 210 prototypes ran into so much trouble (as a result of marked directional instability and a tendency to spin at the slightest provocation) that ErprGr 210 never got its intended aircraft. Instead, production aircraft eventually served with II/ZG 1 on the Eastern Front late in 1941, but the toll of accidents was so great that the aircraft was withdrawn. Modifications were attempted in efforts to cure its ills, and a new unit, Versuchsstaffel 210, was given the task of re-introducing the Me 210 into service in 1942, and a number later saw service in Sicily and the Balkans, but attention had meanwhile switched to the Me 410 (of which more later).

The truly outstanding aircraft that entered service in 1941 was Kurt Tank's Focke-Wulf Fw 190 single-seat, single-engine fighter. This was the only wholly-new combat aircraft introduced into service with the Luftwaffe after the outbreak of war that was to be built in really significant numbers.

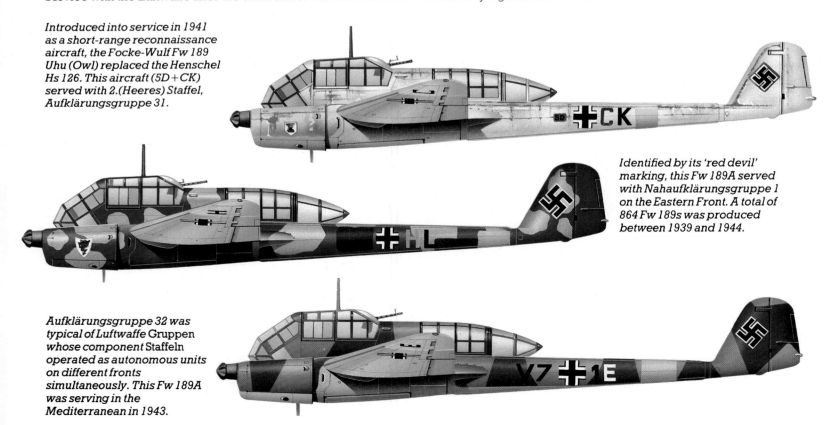

Introduced into service in 1941 as a short-range reconnaissance aircraft, the Focke-Wulf Fw 189 Uhu (Owl) replaced the Henschel Hs 126. This aircraft (5D+CK) served with 2.(Heeres) Staffel, Aufklärungsgruppe 31.

Identified by its 'red devil' marking, this Fw 189A served with Nahaufklärungsgruppe 1 on the Eastern Front. A total of 864 Fw 189s was produced between 1939 and 1944.

Aufklärungsgruppe 32 was typical of Luftwaffe Gruppen whose component Staffeln operated as autonomous units on different fronts simultaneously. This Fw 189A was serving in the Mediterranean in 1943.

The Messerschmitt Me 210 Zerstörer was not considered a success, the variant illustrated here, the Me 210A-1 being armed with two 20-mm and two 7.92-mm (0.31-m) guns. It was superseded by the excellent Me 410.

Having made its first flight on 1 June 1939, the aircraft underwent some alteration before entering production at a number of factories at the end of 1940. Against the widely adopted trend by designers, who favoured the sleek contours made possible by inline liquid-cooled engines, Tank designed the Fw 190 around the bulky but very powerful 14-cylinder BMW 801 air-cooled radial, but produced a superbly compact, low-drag installation that from the outset gave the new fighter a significantly greater top speed than that of the Messerschmitt Bf 109.

The Focke-Wulf Fw 190A first joined the Luftwaffe based in France in August 1941, a fact that has never been satisfactorily explained for, at that time, Germany was mainly preoccupied by a strenuous and vital campaign in the East, and the Bf 109Fs (such as there were) seemed able to cope with the RAF's daylight excursions over France and the Low Countries. As it was, the appearance of the deadly Fw 190 eclipsed the Spitfire Mk V which formed the backbone of RAF Fighter Command, and swung the balance of air superiority in the Luftwaffe's favour. Within six months the new fighter came to provide the principal equipment of JG 2 and JG 26 'Schlageter', and successfully protected the German warships *Scharnhorst, Gneisenau* and *Prinz Eugen* during their spectacular dash up the English Channel in February 1942. The Fw 190 did not join the Luftwaffe for operations on the Eastern Front until March 1942 when, in a reconnaissance version, it joined 9.(H)/LG 2.

The Focke-Wulf Fw 190A (fighter-bombers seen here with centreline bomb racks) came as an unpleasant surprise to the RAF in Western Europe towards the end of 1941, being more than a match for the Spitfire Mk V.

The End of Supremacy

As Allied resources were harnessed to halt the German advances at Stalingrad and Alamein, America entered the war and fortunes changed inexorably against the European Axis powers. Henceforth German air power would be almost entirely geared to defence.

Left: Line-up of Focke-Wulf Fw 190G-3 assault fighter-bombers of 5. Staffel, Schlachtgeschwader 1, Deblin-Irena, Poland, January 1943. Some aircraft are carrying the Mickey Mouse emblem on the engine cowling.

A Junkers Ju 87G armed with two underwing 37-mm anti-tank guns; this version was used to deadly effect against Soviet tanks at the great Battle of Kursk in July 1943, the special ammunition being capable of penetrating a T-34 tank.

In December 1941 the United States of America entered the war against Germany, an event that must have convinced the less fanatically-blinded German leaders that, even if total defeat could be avoided, total victory would be impossible. Already the objective of a quick victory in the East had been compromised by the arrival of the Russian winter. And in North Africa the British were showing themselves generally capable of withstanding the joint armies of Germany and Italy. The Royal Air Force, now equipped with a sizeable force of four-engine Avro Lancasters, Handley Page Halifaxes and Short Stirlings, was beginning to mount devastating attacks on German cities, raids which the Luftwaffe's *Nachtjagdverband* seemed powerless to prevent. Certainly the objective of a victory in Europe within three years seemed to be receding.

Yet it would be some months before the effects of the USA's entry into the war would be felt. In the meantime the Luftwaffe redoubled its efforts to bring into service new, improved aircraft. The total number of *Jagdgruppen,* equipping with new versions of the Bf 109 and Fw 190, rose in six months by 14 with almost 500 extra aircraft; *Stukageschwader* increased by two with more than 200 aircraft, and *Kampfgruppen* by 11 with more than 300 aircraft.

German Warplanes of World War II

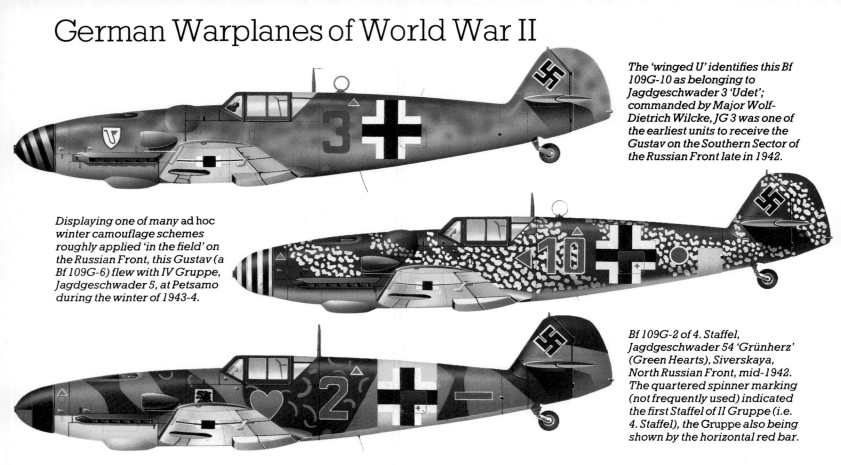

The 'winged U' identifies this Bf 109G-10 as belonging to Jagdgeschwader 3 'Udet'; commanded by Major Wolf-Dietrich Wilcke, JG 3 was one of the earliest units to receive the Gustav on the Southern Sector of the Russian Front late in 1942.

Displaying one of many ad hoc winter camouflage schemes roughly applied 'in the field' on the Russian Front, this Gustav (a Bf 109G-6) flew with IV Gruppe, Jagdgeschwader 5, at Petsamo during the winter of 1943-4.

Bf 109G-2 of 4. Staffel, Jagdgeschwader 54 'Grünherz' (Green Hearts), Siverskaya, North Russian Front, mid-1942. The quartered spinner marking (not frequently used) indicated the first Staffel of II Gruppe (i.e. 4. Staffel), the Gruppe also being shown by the horizontal red bar.

Fighter armament was undergoing rapid change. The old MG FF 20-mm cannon had given place to the faster-firing MG 151/20; the rifle-calibre MG 17 was being overtaken by the 13-mm (0.51-in) MG 131, and the 15-mm machine-gun had entered service. More significant was the appearance of the excellent 30-mm MK 108 cannon which was superior to anything the RAF possessed for knocking down bombers.

All-round improvements

Defensive armament for bombers had also been improved with the introduction of twin MG 81 guns in place of the previous single MG 17s, and with 20-mm guns in movable mountings. Bomb loads were being substantially improved by the introduction of more powerful engines, notably the 1,750-hp (1306-kW) DB 603A and the BMW 801D of similar power; great progress had also been made with water-methanol and nitrous-oxide power boosting, these engines being capable of delivering over 2,000 hp (1492 kW) for short bursts.

In the field of night-fighting, the immediate need was neither for more speed nor for heavier armament but for improvement in airborne radar, and in 1942 the Messerschmitt Bf 110 night-fighters beginning to join the Luftwaffe were equipped with *Lichtenstein BC* or *Lichtenstein C-1*

A Messerschmitt Bf 109G-6 of 7./JG 27 flying escort to a Heinkel He 111 during the Aegean campaign of November 1943; at that time III/JG 27 was based at Athens. The characteristic bulges over the nose gun bodies can be clearly seen.

A short-finned Messerschmitt Bf 109G-14 of IV/JG 53; commanded by Major Günther von Maltzahn, JG 53 was heavily engaged in operations in the Mediterranean during 1943-4, but ultimately components were withdrawn for the defence of Germany.

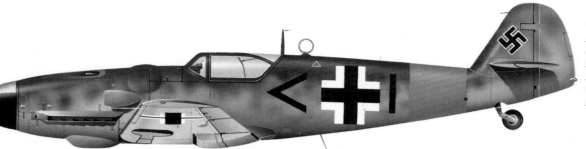

The Messerschmitt Bf 109G-14/R2 fighter-bomber introduced an enlarged wooden fin and rudder to recover lateral stability which had suffered while carrying underfuselage bombs.

radars which had a range of about 2½ miles (4 km). By the end of the year the German night-fighter force amounted to 389 aircraft of which at least 300 were Bf 110s. The *Nachtjagdverband* had, during 1942, destroyed more than 800 RAF bombers.

On the Russian front, 1942 witnessed the German army battle its way to the farthest extent of its eastward advance before being hammered to a halt at Stalingrad. The ferocity of the campaign resulted in enormous losses by both sides, although the Bf 109 and, latterly, the Fw 190 retained their superiority over all Soviet aircraft. British and American aircraft were beginning to arrive in fast-increasing numbers, however, being supplied by convoy round the North Cape and from the Middle East.

The most important fighter to join the Luftwaffe during 1942 was the Messerschmitt Bf 109G (affectionately named the 'Gustav' by German pilots). Powered by a 1,475-hp (1100-kW) DB 605A engine with nitrous-oxide boost, the Bf 109G dispensed with the 7.92-mm (0.31-in) guns, mounting twin 13-mm (0.51-in) guns in addition to a variety of alternative wing guns; the most important variant was the Bf 109G-6 with a hub-firing 30-mm cannon. During 1942 the 'Gustav' joined JG2 in France, JG 1 in Germany, JG 3 and JG 52 in southern Russia, JG 5 in Scandinavia, and JG 27, JG 53 and JG 54 in the Mediterranean. Furthermore, III/JG 54 with Bf 109Gs had been brought home to Germany from the East for defence against the growing daylight attacks by American bombers.

Dieppe

The Focke-Wulf Fw 190A continued to increase in numbers in the West, and by August the excellent Fw 190A-4 fighter-bomber had arrived. In that month the Allies launched their seaborne landing at Dieppe, one of whose aims was to attract the Luftwaffe into the air and to engage it with superior forces of Supermarine Spitfire Mk Vs and Mk IXs (hurriedly introduced to counter the Fw 190) and Hawker Typhoons. In the event neither the Spitfire Mk IX nor the Typhoon were ready in adequate numbers, and were ineffectually committed to battle, while the Spitfire Mk Vs were trounced by the new Fw 190s, which also surprised the Allies with their bombing attacks. All in all, the Dieppe operation proved to be a savage defeat for the RAF.

Also much in evidence at Dieppe was the Dornier Do 217E, which had made a number of heavy raids on Exeter, Norwich, York, Hull, Poole and Grimsby during 1942, and succeeded in carrying

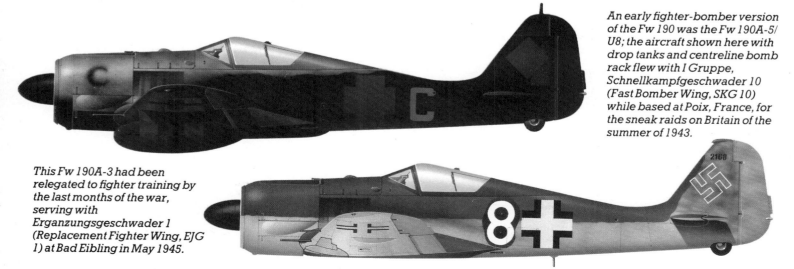

An early fighter-bomber version of the Fw 190 was the Fw 190A-5/U8; the aircraft shown here with drop tanks and centreline bomb rack flew with I Gruppe, Schnellkampfgeschwader 10 (Fast Bomber Wing, SKG 10) while based at Poix, France, for the sneak raids on Britain of the summer of 1943.

This Fw 190A-3 had been relegated to fighter training by the last months of the war, serving with Erganzungsgeschwader 1 (Replacement Fighter Wing, EJG 1) at Bad Eibling in May 1945.

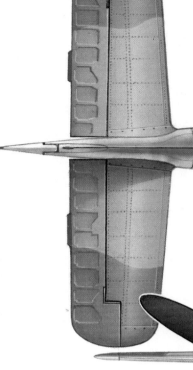

A Focke-Wulf Fw 190G-2 equipped with a centreline ETC 250 bomb rack capable of mounting a single 551-lb (250-kg) bomb; other versions of the Fw 190G could carry bomb loads of up to 3,968 lb (1800 kg).

Focke-Wulf Fw 190

History and Notes

Proposed in 1937, as the Bf 109 was joining the Luftwaffe, Kurt Tank's Focke-Wulf Fw 190 surprisingly featured a bulky air-cooled BMW radial engine. First flown on 1 June 1939, the prototype was followed by short- and long-span pre-production Fw 190A-0s, with BMW 801 14-cylinder radials. The long-span version was selected for production. Fw 190A-1s joined the Luftwaffe in mid-1941 and proved superior to the Spitfire Mk V. A-series variations included the Fw 190A-3 with BMW 801D-2 and two 7.92-mm (0.31-in) and four 20-mm guns, the Fw 190 A-4 with water-methanol power-boosting (with fighter-bomber, bomber-destroyer and tropicalized sub-variants). The Fw 190A-5 featured a slightly lengthened nose and sub-variants included versions with six 30-mm guns (A-5/U12) and torpedo-fighters (A-5/U14 and U15). The Fw 190A-7 and Fw 190A-8 entered production in December 1943 and featured increased armament and armour. The Fw 190A-8/U1 was a two-seat conversion trainer. The next main production version, the Fw 190D, featured a much lengthened nose and Junkers Jumo 213 inline engine in an annular cowling. The Fw 190D-9 was the main service version, which joined the Luftwaffe in the autumn of 1944, and was generally regarded as Germany's best wartime piston-engine fighter; with a top speed of 426 mph (685 km/h), it was armed with two cannon and two machine-guns, and was powered by a water-methanol boosted 2,240-hp (1671-kW) Jumo 213A engine. Other late versions included the Fw 190F and Fw 190G specialized ground-attack fighter-bombers capable of carrying up to 2,250 lb (1000 kg) of bombs.

A development of the Fw 190D was the long-span Focke-Wulf Ta 152 with increased armament and boosted Jumo 213E/B (top speed 472 mph/760 km/h at 41,010 ft/12500 m); a small number of Ta 152H-1s reached the Luftwaffe shortly before the end of the war.

Specification: Focke-Wulf Fw 190A-8
Origin: Germany
Type: single-seat fighter
Powerplant: one 2,100-hp (1567-kW) BMW 801D-2 radial piston engine with water-methanol boosting
Performance: maximum speed 408 mph (654 km/h) at 19,685 ft (6000 m); initial climb rate 2,362 ft (720 m) per minute; service ceiling 37,400 ft (11400 m); normal range 500 miles (805 km)
Weights: empty 6,989 lb (3170 kg); maximum take-off 10,802 lb (4900 kg)
Dimensions: span 34 ft 5½ in (10.50 m); length 29 ft 1½ in (8.84 m); height 13 ft 0 in (3.96 m); wing area 196.98 sq ft (18.30 m²)
Armament: two 7.92-mm (0.31-in) guns on nose and up to four 20-mm guns in wings, plus provision for wide range of underfuselage and underwing bombs, guns and rockets

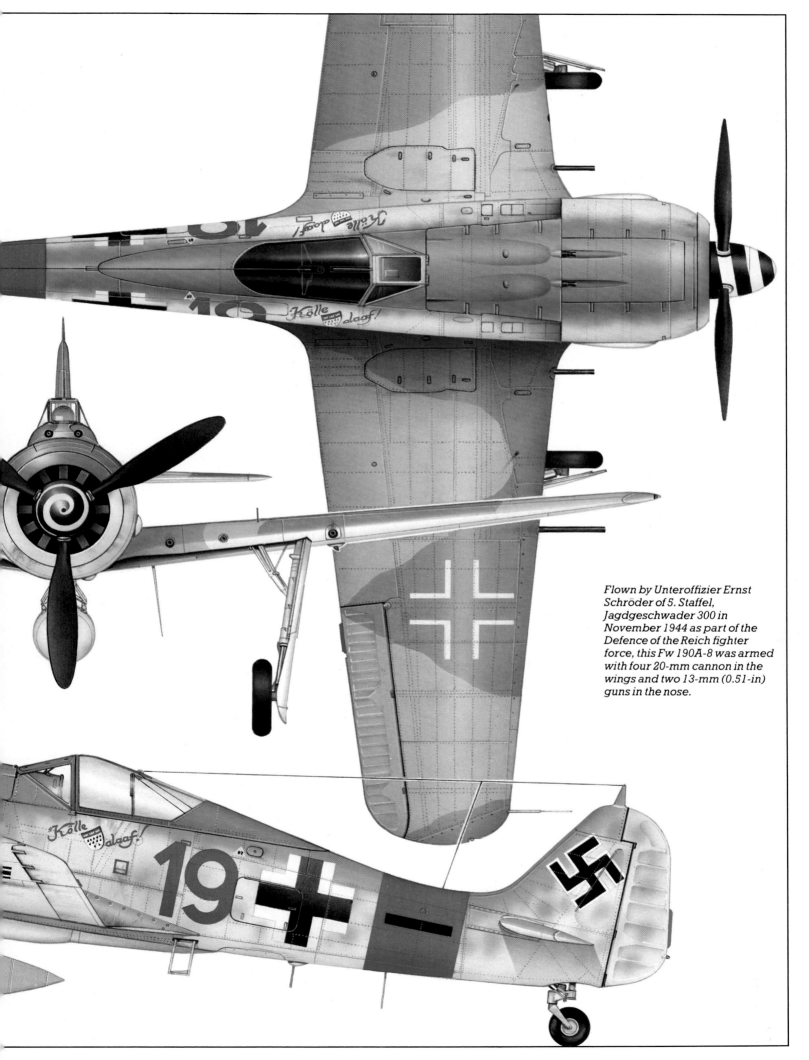

Flown by Unteroffizier Ernst Schröder of 5. Staffel, Jagdgeschwader 300 in November 1944 as part of the Defence of the Reich fighter force, this Fw 190A-8 was armed with four 20-mm cannon in the wings and two 13-mm (0.51-in) guns in the nose.

German Warplanes of World War II

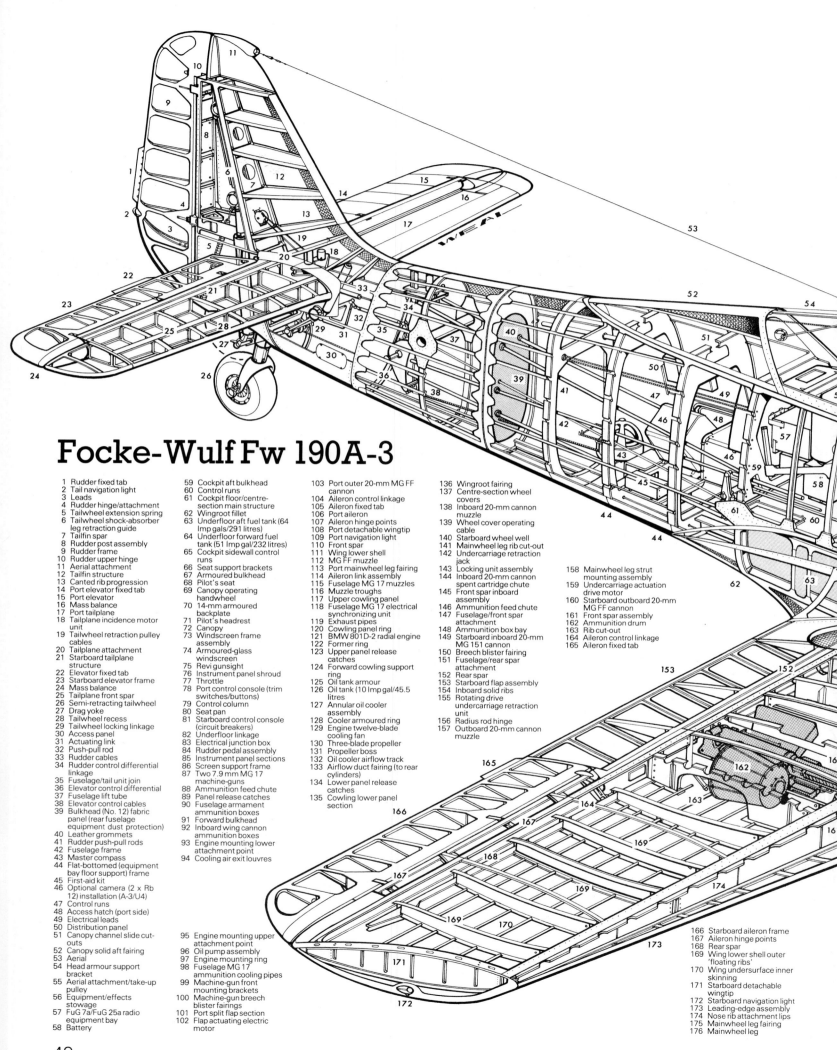

Focke-Wulf Fw 190A-3

1 Rudder fixed tab
2 Tail navigation light
3 Leads
4 Rudder hinge/attachment
5 Tailwheel extension spring
6 Tailwheel shock-absorber leg retraction guide
7 Tailfin spar
8 Rudder post assembly
9 Rudder frame
10 Rudder upper hinge
11 Aerial attachment
12 Tailfin structure
13 Canted rib progression
14 Port elevator fixed tab
15 Port elevator
16 Mass balance
17 Port tailplane
18 Tailplane incidence motor unit
19 Tailwheel retraction pulley cables
20 Tailplane attachment
21 Starboard tailplane structure
22 Elevator fixed tab
23 Starboard elevator frame
24 Mass balance
25 Tailplane front spar
26 Semi-retracting tailwheel
27 Drag yoke
28 Tailwheel recess
29 Tailwheel locking linkage
30 Access panel
31 Actuating link
32 Push-pull rod
33 Rudder cables
34 Rudder control differential linkage
35 Fuselage/tail unit join
36 Elevator control differential
37 Fuselage lift tube
38 Elevator control cables
39 Bulkhead (No. 12) fabric panel (rear fuselage equipment dust protection)
40 Leather grommets
41 Rudder push-pull rods
42 Fuselage frame
43 Master compass
44 Flat-bottomed (equipment bay floor support) frame
45 First-aid kit
46 Optional camera (2 x Rb 12) installation (A-3/U4)
47 Control runs
48 Access hatch (port side)
49 Electrical leads
50 Distribution panel
51 Canopy channel slide cut-outs
52 Canopy solid aft fairing
53 Aerial
54 Head armour support bracket
55 Aerial attachment/take-up pulley
56 Equipment/effects stowage
57 FuG 7a/FuG 25a radio equipment bay
58 Battery

59 Cockpit aft bulkhead
60 Control runs
61 Cockpit floor/centre-section main structure
62 Wingroot fillet
63 Underfloor aft fuel tank (64 Imp gals/291 litres)
64 Underfloor forward fuel tank (51 Imp gal/232 litres)
65 Cockpit sidewall control runs
66 Seat support brackets
67 Armoured bulkhead
68 Pilot's seat
69 Canopy operating handwheel
70 14-mm armoured backplate
71 Pilot's headrest
72 Canopy
73 Windscreen frame assembly
74 Armoured-glass windscreen
75 Revi gunsight
76 Instrument panel shroud
77 Throttle
78 Port control console (trim switches/buttons)
79 Control column
80 Seat pan
81 Starboard control console (circuit breakers)
82 Underfloor linkage
83 Electrical junction box
84 Rudder pedal assembly
85 Instrument panel sections
86 Screen support frame
87 Two 7.9 mm MG 17 machine-guns
88 Ammunition feed chute
89 Panel release catches
90 Fuselage armament ammunition boxes
91 Forward bulkhead
92 Inboard wing cannon ammunition boxes
93 Engine mounting lower attachment point
94 Cooling air exit louvres
95 Engine mounting upper attachment point
96 Oil pump assembly
97 Engine mounting ring
98 Fuselage MG 17 ammunition cooling pipes
99 Machine-gun front mounting brackets
100 Machine-gun breech blister fairings
101 Port split flap section
102 Flap actuating electric motor

103 Port outer 20-mm MG FF cannon
104 Aileron control linkage
105 Aileron fixed tab
106 Port aileron
107 Aileron hinge points
108 Port detachable wingtip
109 Port navigation light
110 Front spar
111 Wing lower shell
112 MG FF muzzle
113 Port mainwheel leg fairing
114 Aileron link assembly
115 Fuselage MG 17 muzzles
116 Muzzle troughs
117 Upper cowling panel
118 Fuselage MG 17 electrical synchronizing unit
119 Exhaust pipes
120 Cowling panel ring
121 BMW 801D-2 radial engine
122 Former ring
123 Upper panel release catches
124 Forward cowling support ring
125 Oil tank armour
126 Oil tank (10 Imp gal/45.5 litres)
127 Annular oil cooler assembly
128 Cooler armoured ring
129 Engine twelve-blade cooling fan
130 Three-blade propeller
131 Propeller boss
132 Oil cooler airflow track
133 Airflow duct fairing (to rear cylinders)
134 Lower panel release catches
135 Cowling lower panel section

136 Wingroot fairing
137 Centre-section wheel covers
138 Inboard 20-mm cannon muzzle
139 Wheel cover operating cable
140 Starboard wheel well
141 Mainwheel leg rib cut-out
142 Undercarriage retraction jack
143 Locking unit assembly
144 Inboard 20-mm cannon spent cartridge chute
145 Front spar inboard assembly
146 Ammunition feed chute
147 Fuselage/front spar attachment
148 Ammunition box bay
149 Starboard inboard 20-mm MG 151 cannon
150 Breech blister fairing
151 Fuselage/rear spar attachment
152 Rear spar
153 Starboard flap assembly
154 Inboard solid ribs
155 Rotating drive undercarriage retraction unit
156 Radius rod hinge
157 Outboard 20-mm cannon muzzle

158 Mainwheel leg strut mounting assembly
159 Undercarriage actuation drive motor
160 Starboard outboard 20-mm MG FF cannon
161 Front spar assembly
162 Ammunition drum
163 Rib cut-out
164 Aileron control linkage
165 Aileron fixed tab

166 Starboard aileron frame
167 Aileron hinge points
168 Rear spar
169 Wing lower shell outer 'floating ribs'
170 Wing undersurface inner skinning
171 Starboard detachable wingtip
172 Starboard navigation light
173 Leading-edge assembly
174 Nose rib attachment lips
175 Mainwheel leg fairing
176 Mainwheel leg

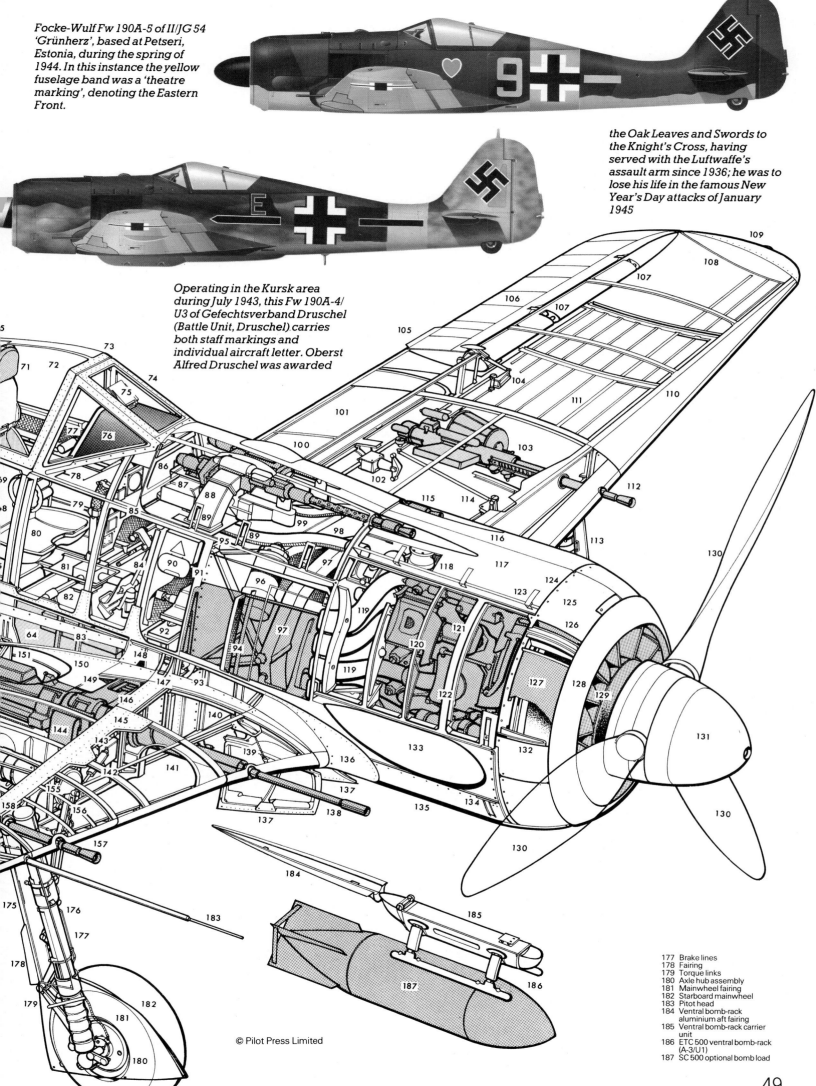

Focke-Wulf Fw 190A-5 of II/JG 54 'Grünherz', based at Petseri, Estonia, during the spring of 1944. In this instance the yellow fuselage band was a 'theatre marking', denoting the Eastern Front.

the Oak Leaves and Swords to the Knight's Cross, having served with the Luftwaffe's assault arm since 1936; he was to lose his life in the famous New Year's Day attacks of January 1945

Operating in the Kursk area during July 1943, this Fw 190A-4/U3 of Gefechtsverband Druschel (Battle Unit, Druschel) carries both staff markings and individual aircraft letter. Oberst Alfred Druschel was awarded

177 Brake lines
178 Fairing
179 Torque links
180 Axle hub assembly
181 Mainwheel fairing
182 Starboard mainwheel
183 Pitot head
184 Ventral bomb-rack aluminium aft fairing
185 Ventral bomb-rack carrier unit
186 ETC 500 ventral bomb-rack (A-3/U1)
187 SC 500 optional bomb load

© Pilot Press Limited

49

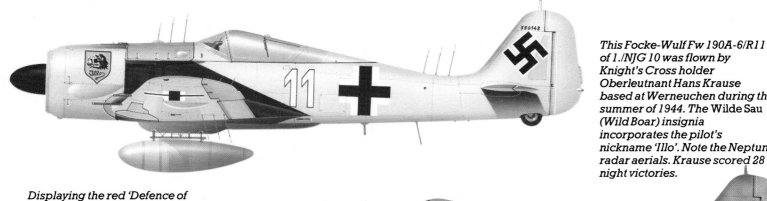

This Focke-Wulf Fw 190A-6/R11 of 1./NJG 10 was flown by Knight's Cross holder Oberleutnant Hans Krause based at Werneuchen during the summer of 1944. The Wilde Sau (Wild Boar) insignia incorporates the pilot's nickname 'Illo'. Note the Neptun radar aerials. Krause scored 28 night victories.

Displaying the red 'Defence of the Reich' fuselage band, this Fw 190A-8 served with I Gruppe, Jagdgeschwader 1, at Twenthe, Holland, in December 1944. The muted fuselage markings were commonplace among Luftwaffe aircraft at this late stage of the war.

Among the many aircraft assembled for Operation Bodenplatte on 1 January 1945 was this Fw 190F-8 fighter-bomber of Schlachtgeschwader 4 flying from Köln-Wahn and Köln-Ostheim. Noted the bulged canopy characteristic of the Fw 190F-series.

out attacks on Allied forces at Dieppe. Ten days later Heinkel He 177A-1s joined in an attack on Bristol, which suffered its worst single incident of the war when a 551-lb (250-kg) bomb dropped from one of these aircraft killed and injured more than 100 people.

Questions in the Mediterranean

It was during 1942 that the Junkers Ju 88 underwent substantial development, much of which was intended to improve its combat potential in the Mediterranean theatre. Junkers Ju 88A-4s of five *Kampfgruppen* were moved to Sicily for operations to eliminate Malta as a British air and naval base, together with a *Gruppe* of Ju 88C intruders for night operations over the island. For some of the raids the bombers carried 2,205-lb (1000-kg) rocket-propelled bombs for attacks on concrete structures. And it was in the numerous heavy attacks on British convoys being sailed to the beleaguered island that the Ju 88 was particularly successful, proving to be too fast for the shipboard Hawker Sea Hurricanes to catch.

A Dornier Do 217E-4. Though a distinct improvement on the much older Do 17, this aircraft suffered problems in its development as a dive bomber, and finished up in the level bombing role. Like so many German bombers it suffered from poor defensive armament.

A Zerstörer (heavy fighter)
version of the Junkers Ju 88 was
the Ju 88C. A Ju 88C-6 (F1+XM)
of 4.(Zerstörer) Staffel,
Kampfgeschwader 76, based at
Taganrog, Ukraine, is shown
here; in an attempt to deceive
enemy pilots the 'solid' nose has
been painted to simulate the
glazed panels of the Ju 88
bomber.

An improved version of the Junkers Ju 87 dive-bomber joined the Luftwaffe at the end of 1941 and thereafter gradually replaced the earlier Ju 87Bs. This was the Ju 87D, powered by the 1,400-hp (1044-kW) Junkers Jumo 211J engine. Obviously little could be done to transform the performance of such a fundamentally 'untidy' aeroplane, although local improvements, including refining the nose shape, improving the rear cockpit and giving the aircraft better armour protection, certainly enhanced it as a weapon. The speed was increased by about 10 mph (16 km/h), but it was in the bombload that the Ju 87D benefitted, it being possible to carry a single 3,968-lb (1800-kg) bomb. Two of the first units to receive the new Stuka were I/StG 2 on the Leningrad front and StG 3 in the Western Desert in May 1942.

Heavy losses (from ground fire and enemy fighters) among the *Stukaverband* resulted in a net decrease in the Luftwaffe's dive-bomber strength during 1942, despite the new deliveries, and it was only by introduction of such aircraft as the ground-attack Henschel Hs 129 (already mentioned) and of the Fw 190 fighter-bomber that adequate close support for the German armies could be afforded. Indeed the entire *Stukaverband* underwent reappraisal, and in May 1942 the new *Schlachtgeschwader* (assault groups) came into being with bomb-carrying Bf 109Fs and Bf 109Gs and the Hs 129; later still the Ju 87 was given an anti-armour attack role, while the Fw 190 replaced it on the *Stukageschwader*, which were in turn renamed *Schlachtfliegergeschwader* (air attack groups) to embrace all ground support and assault forces.

The industry stagnates

As the Axis advance was battered to a standstill at Stalingrad and Alamein, it became clear to the OKL that no longer could German industry be afforded the luxury of time to evolve and introduce wholly new aircraft, and that henceforth the keynote would be improvement and adaptation, and that only improvements which would not seriously jeopardize volume production of existing types could be countenanced. There were of course to be significant exceptions to this policy, as will be seen; but, unlike the British and Americans who were able to introduce such wholly new aircraft as the de Havilland Mosquito, North American Mustang, Hawker Tempest, Republic Thunderbolt and Lockheed Lightning, the backbone of the Luftwaffe up to the end of the war would remain the Fw 190, Bf 109, Do 217, Ju 87 and Ju 88, plus one or two others, such as the Me 410, on the point of entering operational service. By the same token, aircraft which had only recently entered service but which were seen to demand wasteful effort to bring them to anything like worthwhile efficiency would be ruthlessly dropped from production or swiftly relegated to second-line duties.

Bearing the insignia of Luftflotte
2, this Dornier Do 217K-1 was
allocated directly to the Luftflotte
headquarters, and as such was
probably employed for
reconnaissance duties; the Do
217K-1 was normally a night
medium bomber.

Introduced too late to participate in large numbers in the massive tank battles on the Eastern Front of mid-1943, the Ju 87G with two 37-mm anti-tank guns later became the scourge of Russian armour.

Junkers Ju 87

History and Notes
Forever deprecated as a Nazi terror weapon, the Junkers Ju 87 (widely referred to as the Stuka – a contraction of the word *Sturzkampfflugzeug*) was nevertheless an imaginative weapon of considerable accuracy when operating in skies clear of enemy fighters. Conceived as a form of support artillery for the Wehrmacht's *Blitzkrieg* tactics, the Ju 87 was first flown in 1935, a small number of Ju 87A-1s and Ju 87B-1s being flown by the Legion Cóndor in Spain in 1938-9. To support the invasion of Poland the Luftwaffe fielded all five *Stukageschwader* thus far equipped with Ju 87s, and it was in this campaign that, with little effective opposition in the air, the Stuka's legend was born. With sirens screaming, the cranked-wing dive-bombers wrought havoc among Poland's helpless troops and civilians, effectively destroying the country's lines of communication, bridges, railways and airfields. During the difficult Norwegian campaign the Ju 87R with underwing fuel tanks was introduced to cope with the great distances involved, and in the Battle of Britain this version and the Ju 87B were heavily committed until withdrawn temporarily as a result of losses suffered at the hands of British fighter pilots. At the end of 1941 the Ju 87D, a much cleaned-up version with Jumo 211 engine, entered service on the Russian front, and appeared in North Africa the following year. The Ju 87G, a specialist anti-tank aircraft, featured a pair of 37-mm guns under the wings and achieved spectacular success, particularly in the East. Unquestionably the greatest exponent of the Stuka was Hans-Ulrich Rudel whose personal tally of a battleship, a cruiser and a destroyer sunk, and 519 tanks destroyed, far exceeded any other. Total Ju 87 production was said to be 5,709.

Specification: Junkers Ju 87D-7
Origin: Germany
Type: two-seat dive bomber
Powerplant: one 1,500-hp (1119-kW)

Junkers Jumo 211P inline piston engine
Performance: maximum speed 248 mph (400 km/h) at 15,750 ft (4800 m); service ceiling 27,885 ft (8500 m); range 410 miles (660 km)
Weights: empty 8,686 lb (3940 kg); maximum take-off 14,550 lb (6600 kg)
Dimensions: span 49 ft 2½ in (15.00 m); length 37 ft 8¾ in (11.50 m); height 12 ft 9½ in (3.90 m); wing area 362.7 sq ft (33.60 m²)

Armament: two forward-firing 20-mm MG 151/20 cannon and two 7.92-mm (0.31-in) MG 81 machine-guns in the rear cockpit, plus a bombload of one 3,968-lb (1800-kg) bomb under the fuselage and two 1,102-lb (500-kg) bombs under the wings

This Junkers Ju 87G-1 is shown in the markings of 5. Staffel, Schlachtfliegergeschwader 3 (Assault Wing 3), spring 1944. SG 3's II Gruppe was at this time commanded by Major 'Theo' Nordmann, a brilliant Stuka veteran who won the Swords and Oak Leaves to the Knight's Cross and who, by the date of his death on 19 January 1945, had flown 1,200 combat missions as an assault and dive bomber pilot.

German Warplanes of World War II

The codes T6+BH identify this Ju 87D-3 as belonging to 1. Staffel, Stukageschwader 2 'Immelmann', perhaps the most famous of all Stukastaffeln, commanded as it was from November 1942 by Hans-Ulrich Rudel. Rudel, who died in 1982, was the most highly decorated of all German servicemen, flew 2,530 combat missions and was credited with the destruction of 519 Russian tanks.

Junkers Ju 87D-3

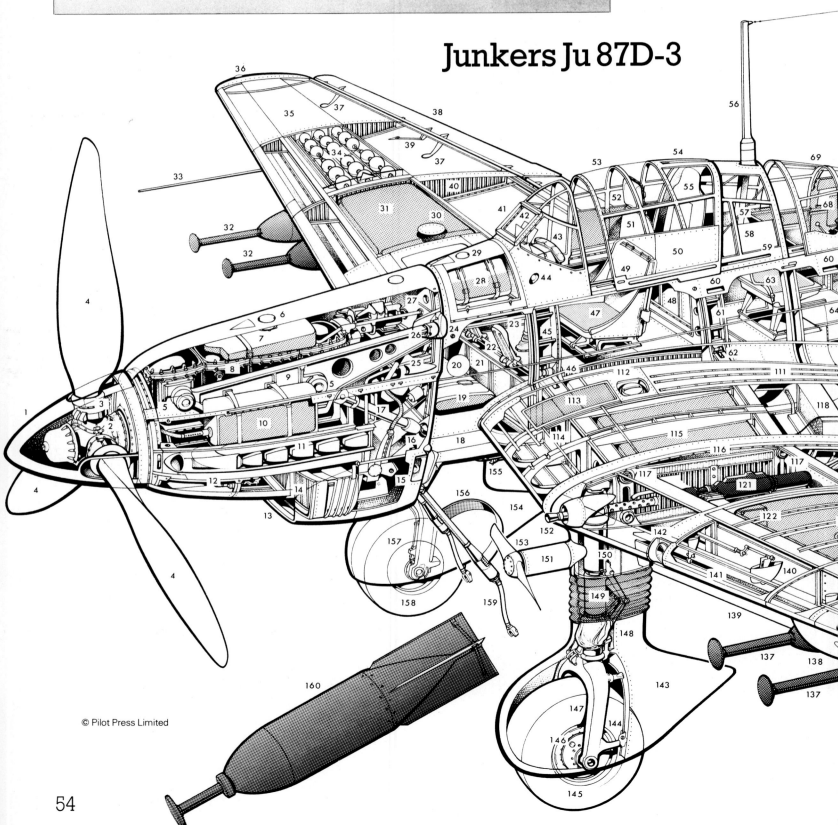

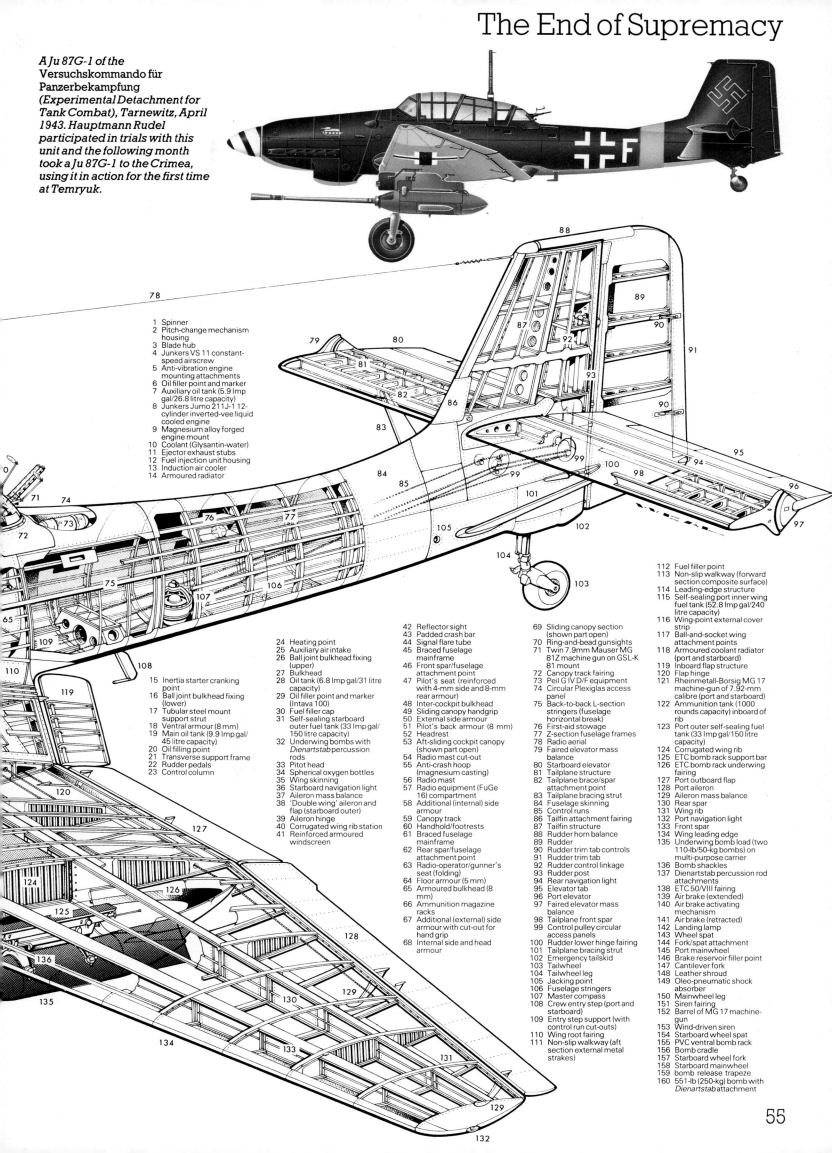

A Ju 87G-1 of the Versuchskommando für Panzerbekampfung (Experimental Detachment for Tank Combat), Tarnewitz, April 1943. Hauptmann Rudel participated in trials with this unit and the following month took a Ju 87G-1 to the Crimea, using it in action for the first time at Temryuk.

1 Spinner
2 Pitch-change mechanism housing
3 Blade hub
4 Junkers VS 11 constant-speed airscrew
5 Anti-vibration engine mounting attachments
6 Oil filler point and marker
7 Auxiliary oil tank (5.9 Imp gal/26.8 litre capacity)
8 Junkers Jumo 211J-1 12-cylinder inverted-vee liquid cooled engine
9 Magnesium alloy forged engine mount
10 Coolant (Glysantin-water)
11 Ejector exhaust stubs
12 Fuel injection unit housing
13 Induction air cooler
14 Armoured radiator

15 Inertia starter cranking point
16 Ball joint bulkhead fixing (lower)
17 Tubular steel mount support strut
18 Ventral armour (8 mm)
19 Main oil tank (9.9 Imp gal/45 litre capacity)
20 Oil filling point
21 Transverse support frame
22 Rudder pedals
23 Control column

24 Heating point
25 Auxiliary air intake
26 Ball joint bulkhead fixing (upper)
27 Bulkhead
28 Oil tank (6.8 Imp gal/31 litre capacity)
29 Oil filler point and marker (Intava 100)
30 Fuel filler cap
31 Self-sealing starboard outer fuel tank (33 Imp gal/150 litre capacity)
32 Underwing bombs with *Dienartstab* percussion rods
33 Pitot head
34 Spherical oxygen bottles
35 Wing skinning
36 Starboard navigation light
37 Aileron mass balance
38 'Double wing' aileron and flap (starboard outer)
39 Aileron hinge
40 Corrugated wing rib station
41 Reinforced armoured windscreen

42 Reflector sight
43 Padded crash bar
44 Signal flare tube
45 Braced fuselage mainframe
46 Front spar/fuselage attachment point
47 Pilot's seat (reinforced with 4-mm side and 8-mm rear armour)
48 Inter-cockpit bulkhead
49 Sliding canopy handgrip
50 External side armour
51 Pilot's back armour (8 mm)
52 Headrest
53 Aft-sliding cockpit canopy (shown part open)
54 Radio mast cut-out
55 Anti-crash hoop (magnesium casting)
56 Radio mast
57 Radio equipment (FuGe 16) compartment
58 Additional (internal) side armour
59 Canopy track
60 Handhold/footrests
61 Braced fuselage mainframe
62 Rear spar/fuselage attachment point
63 Radio-operator/gunner's seat (folding)
64 Floor armour (5 mm)
65 Armoured bulkhead (8 mm)
66 Ammunition magazine racks
67 Additional (external) side armour with cut-out for hand grip
68 Internal side and head armour

69 Sliding canopy section (shown part open)
70 Ring-and-bead gunsights
71 Twin 7.9mm Mauser MG 81Z machine-gun on GSL-K 81 mount
72 Canopy track fairing
73 Peil G IV D/F equipment
74 Circular Plexiglas access panel
75 Back-to-back L-section stringers (fuselage horizontal break)
76 First-aid stowage
77 Z-section fuselage frames
78 Faired elevator mass balance
79 Starboard elevator
80 Starboard elevator
81 Tailplane structure
82 Tailplane brace/spar attachment point
83 Tailplane bracing strut
84 Fuselage skinning
85 Control runs
86 Tailfin attachment fairing
87 Tailfin structure
88 Rudder horn balance
89 Rudder
90 Rudder trim tab controls
91 Rudder trim tab
92 Rudder control linkage
93 Rudder post
94 Rear navigation light
95 Elevator tab
96 Port elevator
97 Faired elevator mass balance
98 Tailplane front spar
99 Control pulley circular access panels
100 Rudder lower hinge fairing
101 Tailplane bracing strut
102 Emergency tailskid
103 Tailwheel
104 Tailwheel leg
105 Jacking point
106 Fuselage stringers
107 Master compass
108 Crew entry step (port and starboard)
109 Entry step support (with control run cut-outs)
110 Wing root fairing
111 Non-slip walkway (aft section external metal strakes)

112 Fuel filler point
113 Non-slip walkway (forward section composite surface)
114 Leading-edge structure
115 Self-sealing port inner wing fuel tank (52.8 Imp gal/240 litre capacity)
116 Wing-point external cover strip
117 Ball-and-socket wing attachment points
118 Armoured coolant radiator (port and starboard)
119 Inboard flap structure
120 Flap hinge
121 Rheinmetall-Borsig MG 17 machine-gun of 7.92-mm calibre (port and starboard)
122 Ammunition tank (1000 rounds capacity) inboard of rib
123 Port outer self-sealing fuel tank (33 Imp gal/150 litre capacity)
124 Corrugated wing rib
125 ETC bomb rack support bar
126 ETC bomb rack underwing fairing
127 Port outboard flap
128 Port aileron
129 Aileron mass balance
130 Rear spar
131 Wing rib
132 Port navigation light
133 Front spar
134 Wing leading edge
135 Underwing bomb load (two 110-lb/50-kg bombs) on multi-purpose carrier
136 Bomb shackles
137 Dienartstab percussion rod attachments
138 ETC 50/VIII fairing
139 Air brake (extended)
140 Air brake activating mechanism
141 Air brake (retracted)
142 Landing lamp
143 Wheel spat
144 Fork/spat attachment
145 Port mainwheel
146 Brake reservoir filler point
147 Cantilever fork
148 Leather shroud
149 Oleo-pneumatic shock absorber
150 Mainwheel leg
151 Siren fairing
152 Barrel of MG 17 machine-gun
153 Wind-driven siren
154 Starboard wheel spat
155 PVC ventral bomb rack
156 Bomb cradle
157 Starboard wheel fork
158 Starboard mainwheel
159 bomb release trapeze
160 551-lb (250-kg) bomb with *Dienartstab* attachment

Ever more frequently, the best German fighters appeared on Allied camera-gun film during the last two years of the war. Here a Focke-Wulf Fw 190 is struck by cannon fire moments before the pilot baled out.

Enemy Pressure Grows

Ringed on almost every side by growing enemy forces, and deprived of Italy's doubtful war effort, Germany faced the spectre of defeat as the Allied air offensive was mounted both against her armies in the field and with ever-increasing intensity against her cities.

Throughout the last 30 months of the war, Germany was almost entirely on the defensive. The European mainland was by 1943 under constant air attack by the Americans in daylight and by RAF Bomber Command at night. At last the British had evolved (by means of pathfinding techniques and the bomber stream) methods by which huge fleets of heavy bombers could reach and strike German towns and cities, while heavily armed formations of American Boeing B-17s and Consolidated B-24s were beginning to strike with great accuracy relatively small key targets deep inside Europe.

To counter the night raids the Luftwaffe continued to strengthen its night-fighter defences and in August 1943 introduced a simple but devastatingly effective new weapon, the *schräge Musik* (shrill music, or jazz) installation of a pair of upward-firing cannon (usually 20-mm) mounted amidships in Messerschmitt Bf 110G-4/R8s and, later, Junkers Ju 88G-6bs. The tactics involved overtaking the

The Luftwaffe came to depend upon the use of gliders for heavy-lift supply on the Eastern Front. Here a Messerschmitt Me 321 Gigant glider is towed off the ground by three Bf 110 fighters.

Heinkel He 219

History and Notes
Without doubt the best German night-fighter of the war, the He 219 possessed in abundance all three attributes essential for such combat – high speed, heavy gun armament and efficient radar. The He 219 V1 was flown on 15 November 1942 and production examples would have followed quickly thereafter had an RAF raid on Rostock not destroyed more than three-quarters of the design drawings. Pre-production He 219A-0s were delivered to NJG1 at Venlo in April 1943, and on the first combat sortie Major Werner Streib destroyed five Lancasters within 30 minutes on 11-12 June. The first version to be produced in quantity was the He 219A-5 with two 30-mm and two 20-mm cannon. At the end of 1943 the He 219 was officially abandoned on the ground that the Ju 88G was capable of catching the Lancaster and Halifax, but as the He 219 was the only night-fighter able to deal with the Mosquito, production continued at a reduced rate. The major variant, the He 219A-7, was introduced in 1944, the He 279 A-7/R1 armed with no fewer than eight cannon – four forward-firing 30-mm and two of 20-mm, plus two upward-firing 30-mm guns in a *schräge Musik* installation. Fastest of all the He 219A series versions was the He 219A-7/R6 with 2,500-hp (1865-kW) Jumo 222A/B engines and a top speed of 435 mph (700 km/h). Most aircraft were equipped with FuG 220 *Lichtenstein* SN-2 radar. It has been estimated that of all RAF Mos-

A Heinkel He 219A (G9+FH) of I/NJG 1, the first unit to fly the He 219 on operations. The CO, Major Werner Streib, shot down five Lancasters in 30 minutes on the night of 11/12 June 1944.

quitoes lost during night operations more than 60 per cent fell to He 219s – this despite the fact that production of the Uhu (Owl) amounted to no more than 268 aircraft.

Specification: Heinkel He 219A-7/R1 Uhu
Origin: Germany
Type: two-seat high-altitude night-fighter
Powerplant: two 1,800-hp (1343-kW)

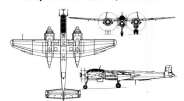

Heinkel He 219A-5R1

Daimler Benz DB 603E inline piston engines
Performance: maximum speed 416 mph (670 km/h) at 22,965 ft (7000 m); initial climb rate 1,805 ft (550 m) per minute; absolute ceiling 41,665 ft (1270 m); range 1,243 miles (2000 km)
Weights: empty 24,691 lb (11200 kg); loaded 33,730 lb (15300 kg)

Dimensions: span 60 ft 8½ in (18.50 m); length 50 ft 11¾ in (15.54 m); height 13 ft 5½ in (4.10 m); wing area 479.0 sq ft (44.50 m²)
Armament: two 30-mm MK 108 cannon in wing roots, two 30-mm MK 103 and two 20-mm MG 151/20 cannon in ventral gun tray, and two upward-firing 30-mm Mk 108 cannon in rear cockpit

By no means an attractive aeroplane, the Heinkel He 219 was undoubtedly one of the best night fighters of the war.

night bomber from the rear and attacking from beneath (where there were no defensive guns), firing upwards into the engines and fuel tanks. For many months, while the very existence of the new weapon was scarcely suspected by the British, casualties increased rapidly and a number of German *Experten* (aces) were frequently adding four, five or more four-engine bombers to their victory tallies on single nights.

Night-fighter developments

A new and deadly night fighter started appearing in the *Nachtjagdgeschwader* in 1943. This was the Heinkel He 219 with DB 603A engines and a top speed of 416 mph (670 km/h), and armed with two 30-mm and two 20-mm cannon. The He 219 had narrowly escaped being axed during the reappraisal of new German projects, but survived when it was pointed out that it was the only night-fighter capable of catching the de Havilland Mosquito, which was by 1943 appearing in increasing numbers in the night skies over Germany.

More significant were the improvements being made in German airborne radar, and by 1943 most Bf 110s, Ju 88s and He 219s were equipped with the FuG 212 *Lichtenstein C-1* with prominent

The Heinkel He 219A-053 was used as a prototype for the He 219A-5/R1 (the first production version); it carried an armament of two 20-mm and two 30-mm cannon and proved easily capable of knocking down RAF night bombers in large numbers.

Spanning 180 feet (55 m), the Messerschmitt Me 321 Gigant was by far the largest glider produced during the war; an aircraft is seen here landing, its wheel undercarriage having previously been jettisoned after take-off.

'toasting fork' aerial array on the nose. The first major setback for the Luftwaffe night defences occurred on the night of 24/25 July 1943 when the RAF started dropping 'Window', codename for huge quantities of small metallized foil strips cut to half the wavelength of German radar. Within moments the entire screen provided by ground *Würzburg* and airborne *Lichtenstein* radars had been blinded by spurious signals. This was but another weapon in the growing armoury of radio countermeasures warfare, and led the Germans to adopt a number of expedients, including the use of day fighters on freelance night patrols for visual interception (not being dependent on radar), and the 'insertion' of Bf 110s into the bomber stream for visual attacks; the former (*wilde Sau*, wild boar) tactics proved to be very effective on moonlit nights, and the latter (*zahme Sau*, tame boar) worthwhile in the area of the target where ground fires silhouetted the British bombers.

By day the *Jagdverband* was using every available fighter to attack the big American bomber formations. It had been discovered early on that the B-17 and B-24 were relatively poorly armed in the nose, with the result that the favourite method of attack, though demanding nerves of steel, was the head-on pass, and the fast-firing 15-mm and 20-mm cannon of the Messerschmitt Bf 109Gs and Focke-Wulf Fw 190A-5s were extremely effective. A new version of the latter was the Fw 190A-6 which could mount a battery of six 20-mm cannon, while the Fw 190A-6/R6 could carry a single 21-cm (8.3-in) rocket under each wing. Bf 110s, Junkers Ju 88s and Dornier Do 217s were also introduced as bomber-destroyers with large calibre weapons, and there were even plans to introduce such improbable aircraft as the Heinkel He 177 (as the He 177A-5) in the *Zerstörer* role, each with 33 upward-firing rockets. Among the novel, though not particularly successful, tactics was the aerial bombing of American bomber formations by Bf 109Gs and Fw 190s carrying 551-lb

Powered version of the Me 321 glider was the six-engine Me 323, seen here taking off with the aid of six auxiliary rocket units under the wings in addition to its six Gnome-Rhône radials.

German Warplanes of World War II

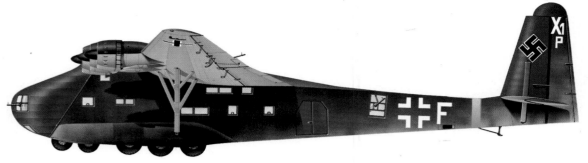

(250-kg) bombs, the first American bomber being destroyed in this manner on 22 March 1943.

An early milestone in the daylight defence against American bombers was reached on 17 August 1943 when more than 300 Bf 109s, Bf 110s, Fw 190s, Me 210s and Ju 88s intercepted a similar number of American bombers and destroyed 60 of them, damaging 100 others. On 14 October 228 bombers attacked the ball-bearing factories at Schweinfurt, losing 79 of their number shot down and 121 damaged by the German defences. It was at this point, with losses far outstripping the replacement rate, that the decision was taken to introduce American long-range fighter escorts, but it was some time before the superlative North American P-51 Mustang (which could accompany the bombers all the way to Berlin and back) could be brought into service.

Hit-and-run

Meanwhile the Fw 190A was being employed in a new role over the British Isles, that of daylight hit-and-run raider. A new unit, SKG10 (*Schnellkampfgeschwader* or fast bomber group), was flying Fw 190A-4/U8s with a 1,102-lb (500-kg) bomb under the fuselage and underwing drop tanks. Heavy damage was done in such raids on London, Eastbourne, Canterbury, Hastings and Ashford, and caused RAF Fighter Command to deploy quite disproportionate fighter strength to counter raids by seldom more than about a dozen Focke-Wulfs.

In North Africa and the Mediterranean, 1943 was a disastrous year for the Axis. After a period in which the Bf 109F and Bf 109G gained the upper hand, before the 2nd Battle of Alamein (when a young German pilot, Hauptmann Hans-Joachim Marseille, became the highest-scoring fighter pilot against the Western Allies with 158 air victories before being killed in an accident in a Bf 109G on 30 September 1942), the build-up of overwhelming Allied air strength crushed the Luftwaffe and Regia Aeronautica. By the time the Axis armies had been crowded into the northern tip of Tunisia early in 1943, the Luftwaffe was almost powerless. Even when in June two *Gruppen* (II and IV/SKG 10) of Fw 190A-4/U8s were transferred from France to Sicily, they proved unable to affect the course of battle. Desperate measures were adopted to supply fuel and ammunition to the Axis forces in Tunisia, unescorted formations of Junker Ju 52/3ms and the huge six-engine Messerschmitt Me 323 transports being flown across the Sicilian narrows in daylight. On more than one occasion these formations were spotted by Allied fighter pilots who knocked them into the sea with consummate ease. The Me 323 transport was capable of carrying 130 troops (or more in an emergency) and had been developed from the Me 321 Gigant (Giant) glider principally as a supply aircraft for moving

A Junkers Ju 188D-2 photo reconnaissance aircraft of 1.(F)/124, equipped with FuG 200 search radar and based at Kirkenes in northern Norway during 1944. This unit provided intelligence about Allied North Cape convoys for torpedo operations by KG 26.

men and matériel on the Eastern Front, and was typical of the expedients being adopted by Germany at this stage of the war. Significantly it was never intended as an assault glider in the same concept as the British Airspeed Horsa and General Aircraft Hamilcar gliders. It is worth mentioning in passing here that for towing the huge Me 321 glider the Luftwaffe began by using trios of Bf 110s but later produced the extraordinary Heinkel He 111Z Zwilling (Twin); this was in effect a pair of He 111 bombers joined together with a new centre wing on which a fifth engine was added.

Missile pioneering

Before leaving the war in the Mediterranean, one other aspect of Luftwaffe operations should be mentioned, namely the successful introduction of the radio-controlled rocket-assisted glider bombs, of which the Henschel Hs 293 was the best known. This missile consisted of a winged bomb, powered by a Walter 109 liquid-fuel rocket. Weighing 2,304 lb (1045 kg), of which 1,102 lb (500 kg) was explosive, one Hs 293 was carried under the wing of the Do 217E-5, and entered service with II/KG 40 and II/KG 100 on the west coast of France in August 1943. These units were transferred to the south of France in the following month and were used to no mean effect against Allied shipping in the Mediterranean, particularly during the Anzio landings. Hs 293As were also carried by He 111H-12s, by He 177A-3s and He 177A-5s, by Fw 200Cs, and by Do 217Ks, Do 217Ms and Do 217Rs.

Another missile used with success was the controlled-trajectory armour-piercing X-1 *Fritz X* bomb of 3,461 lb (1570 kg); these bombs were first carried by aircraft of III/KG 100, this unit being responsible for the sinking of the battleship *Roma* after Italy's capitulation in September 1943.

In northern Europe a new medium bomber joined in operations against the UK. This was the Junkers Ju 188, an extensively redesigned development of the excellent Ju 88 which, in the interests of maximum production had itself been changed very little in four years. The Ju 188, powered initially by two 1,600-hp (1194-kW) BMW 801L and later by 1,700-hp (1268-KW) BMW 801D or G

After the four-engine prototype Messerschmitt Me 323 was found to be underpowered, six Gnome-Rhône radials were fitted in the Me 323V2 (second prototype) shown here. Structure of this huge aircraft was of welded steel tubing and wood, with fabric and wood covering.

German Warplanes of World War II

One of the first units to receive the Messerschmitt Me 410A Hornisse (Hornet) was III Gruppe, Zerstörergeschwader 1, in May 1943. This Me 410A-1 was flown by 9. Staffel from Gerbini.

engines, had a top speed of 311 mph (500 km/h), which was not much more than the Ju 88, but could carry a bombload of up to 6,614 lb (3000 kg) or two torpedoes. With sharply pointed wings the German aircraft also appeared in reconnaissance form on the Russian front in 1943, and underwent continuous development right up to the end of the war, culminating in such versions as the Ju 188S-1/U close-support aircraft with 50-mm anti-tank cannon, and the Ju 188T, a 435-mph (700-km/h) reconnaissance version.

The final 'Zerstörer'

As already stated, the Messerschmitt Me 210 had proved a failure in service, and this aircraft was one of the casualties of the swingeing cuts imposed on Luftwaffe projects in 1942; a radical development, the Me 310, was also abandoned in favour of the Me 410, which gave much better promise. Powered by DB 603A engines in lengthened nacelles, the Me 410 Hornisse (Hornet) entered service in Germany and Italy in May 1943 with bomber, reconnaissance and *Zerstörer Gruppen* simultaneously. With a top speed of 388 mph (625 km/h) the new aircraft proved a tough opponent, and versions existed which could carry two 2,205-lb (1000-kg) bombs internally, or were armed with a single 50-mm gun or combinations of 30-mm, 20-mm and 15-mm guns. Me 410s were particularly active in raids over the UK during 1943-4, proving capable of being caught only by Mosquito night-fighters.

The inexorable turn of fortune for the German forces in the East, following the debacle at Stalingrad, was accompanied by greatly increased pressure on the Luftwaffe. By the spring of 1943 the fruits of Russian industrial expansion for war purposes were evidenced with huge deliveries of such aircraft as the Ilyushin Il-2 *Shtormovik* ground-support aircraft but, more significantly, by the

The excellent Messerschmitt Me 410, which entered service in 1943, was produced to perform a number of different duties. This Me 410A-3 (F6+WK) of 2. Staffel, Aufklärungsgruppe 122, was based at Trapani in May 1943.

The ugly Arado Ar 232B-0 was a four-engine development of the twin-engine Ar 232A of which only prototypes were produced. Nicknamed Tausendfüssler (Millipedes), a small number of aircraft served on special duties on the Eastern Front in 1944; the aircraft shown was flown by Transport-Staffel 5.

appearance of the Lavochkin La 5, an excellent radial-engine fighter of similar appearance and performance to the Fw 190. Henceforth the Soviet forces would exercise an initiative to select their own battlegrounds and apply sufficient strength to overwhelm the local German forces. These tactics imposed considerable strain upon the Luftwaffe's air supply units, and all manner of improvisation was undertaken to bolster the overworked *Transportgruppen*. The Heinkel He 111, by now recognized as being slow and vulnerable as a bomber, was pressed into service as a transport. It was first used as such during the Stalingrad operations, ancient He 111D and He 111F versions being joined by the He 111P and He 111H. Nevertheless, in the face of local Soviet air superiority, casualties were very heavy, no fewer than 165 He 111s being lost in little over a month. Among other aircraft pressed into use as transports to join the Ju 52/3m, Me 323 and Ju 90 were the

Bearing a diminutive form of the wasp insignia, this Me 410 B-2/U2/R4 belonged to Zerstörergeschwader 1; the R4 conversion pack increased the forward armament of this version to eight 20-mm cannon.

German Warplanes of World War II

A Gotha Go 244B wearing the markings of 4./KGrzbV 106 early in 1943; by this time however the unit had almost entirely re-equipped with the Ju 52/3m.

Arado Ar 232, Focke-Wulf Fw 200, Gotha Go 244 (a powered version of the Go 242 glider), Junkers Ju 252, Ju 290 and Ju 352, and Messerschmitt Me 264; most of these aircraft existed only in prototype or pre-production form.

New tactics in the East

In the great armoured Battle of Kursk of July 1943 the pattern of future ground-support operations was set. The advent of the excellent Russian T-34 tank in huge numbers brought about the creation of *Schlachtfliegergeschwader* (already mentioned) equipped primarily with the Fw 190 in assault-fighter form, and other ad hoc units, such as armoured-fighter *Staffeln* within fighter groups (for example PzJäg/JG 51 'Mölders'). An offshoot of this new tactical concept was the development of the Night Assault Groups (*Nachtschlachtgeschwader*) whose task was to range over and behind the Soviet lines dropping light bombs and causing widespread disorganization. In due course about 15 such *Geschwader* were formed, not all on the Eastern Front, and flew an extraordinary variety of aircraft including the Arado Ar 66, Caproni Ca 314, Dornier Do 17, Fiat CR.42, Focke-Wulf Fw 158, Fokker C-V, Gotha Go 145, Henschel Hs 126, Heinkel He 46 and 50, Polikarpov Po-2 and Siebel Si 204.

By early 1944, as an Allied landing in western Europe obviously appeared imminent, as the Allies fought their way northwards in Italy and as Russia gradually beat back the German armies in the East, the Western air forces were piling on the agony from the air over the homeland. The perimeter of the Third Reich was now beginning to shrink, and the spectre of assault from enemies on all sides was now a reality.

A Gotha Go 244B-1 powered glider. Aircraft of this type were used by KGrzbV 104 in Greece and KGrzbV 106 in Crete during 1942, but when flown in North Africa were very vulnerable to anti-aircraft fire and were quickly withdrawn.

A ground view of a Go 244B-3 showing the non-jettisonable landing gear and the upward-hinged rear loading door. The Go 244 was capable of carrying a Kübelwagen and six to eight troops.

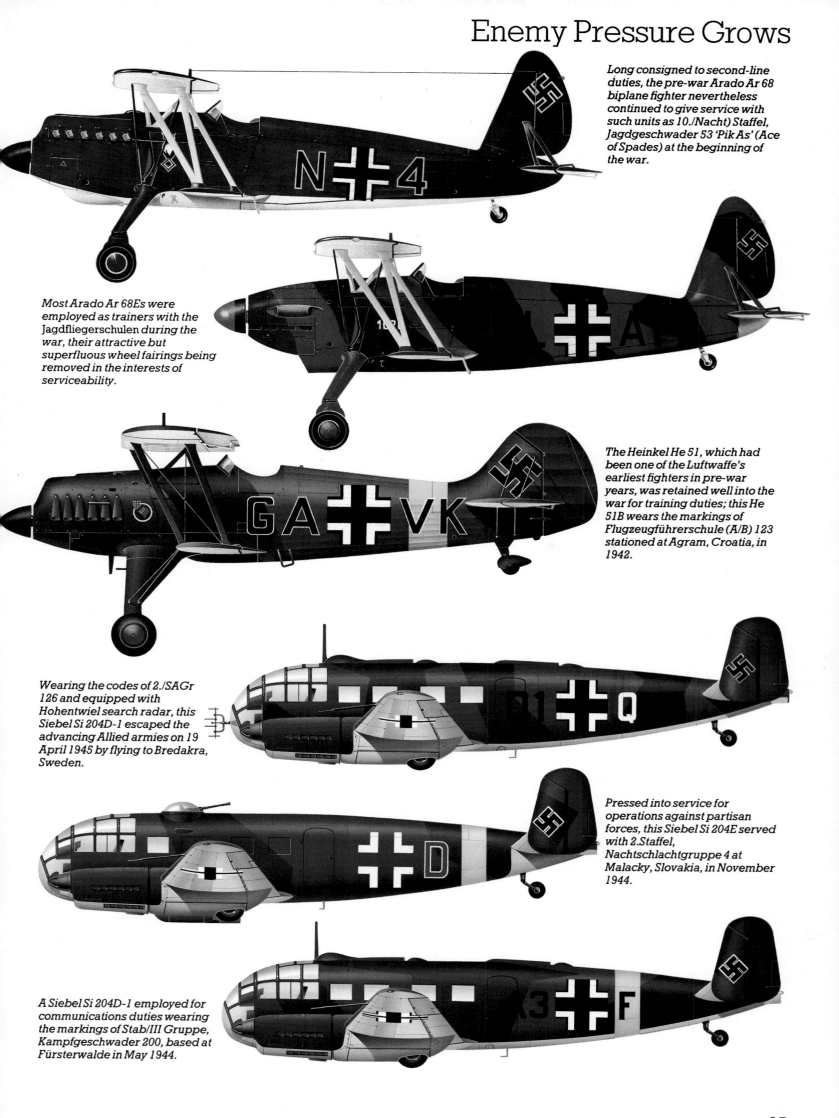

Long consigned to second-line duties, the pre-war Arado Ar 68 biplane fighter nevertheless continued to give service with such units as 10./Nacht) Staffel, Jagdgeschwader 53 'Pik As' (Ace of Spades) at the beginning of the war.

Most Arado Ar 68Es were employed as trainers with the Jagdfliegerschulen during the war, their attractive but superfluous wheel fairings being removed in the interests of serviceability.

The Heinkel He 51, which had been one of the Luftwaffe's earliest fighters in pre-war years, was retained well into the war for training duties; this He 51B wears the markings of Flugzeugführerschule (A/B) 123 stationed at Agram, Croatia, in 1942.

Wearing the codes of 2./SAGr 126 and equipped with Hohentwiel search radar, this Siebel Si 204D-1 escaped the advancing Allied armies on 19 April 1945 by flying to Bredakra, Sweden.

Pressed into service for operations against partisan forces, this Siebel Si 204E served with 2.Staffel, Nachtschlachtgruppe 4 at Malacky, Slovakia, in November 1944.

A Siebel Si 204D-1 employed for communications duties wearing the markings of Stab/III Gruppe, Kampfgeschwader 200, based at Fürsterwalde in May 1944.

Despite its heavy armament and greatly superior speed, the Messerschmitt Me 262 jet fighter was on several occasions engaged and shot down by Allied fighters (such as the P-51 Mustang and Hawker Tempest); this is a camera-gun frame from a USAAF P-51 Mustang.

Defence of the Reich

With British, American and Russian armies closing in on the frontiers of the German homeland, the Luftwaffe was forced to concentrate on desperate measures to combat the great bombing armadas that threatened to pulverize city after city into smoking rubble.

While the realists among Germany's air defence planners pressed for single-minded concentration upon the best Luftwaffe fighters, the Nazi leaders still pinned their faith on miraculous terror and retaliation weapons. At the beginning of 1944 development still continued of a huge six-engine bomber, the Junkers Ju 390 (which during trials reached to within 12 miles/20 km of New York before returning safely to its base in France); but even this was abandoned in favour of weapons to strike at targets nearer at hand.

When the Allies eventually launched their great invasion in Normandy in June 1944, there were inadequate Luftwaffe forces on the spot to dispute air superiority, most of the bombers in France being deployed for maritime operations over the Atlantic. Rapid redeployment brought together about 16 *Gruppen* of Fw 190As, including some of the new armoured-assault Focke-Wulf Fw 190 A-8/R7s of IV (Stürm)/JG 3, and several of Messerschmitt Bf 109Gs. Reconnaissance over the invasion area was undertaken by Bf 109G-8s of 3./NAGr 12. In due course German bombers began attempts to attack the swiftly expanding beachhead, Hs 293-armed Dornier Do 217s attacking a number of key bridges, but British and American air attacks had already destroyed most of the

The Focke-Wulf Ta 152 was only appearing in numbers in the very last weeks of the war; illustrated here is the Ta 152CV7 which was flown in March 1945. Top speed was in the region of 435 mph (700 km/h).

Junkers Ju 88s and Junkers Ju 188s on their French bases.

Meanwhile a new form or air warfare was being introduced with the launching of the Fieseler Fi 103 (or V1) flying-bombs against southern England (and later Paris and Brussels). Development of these unmanned, pulse jet-powered missiles had gone ahead for almost two years in the face of Allied air attacks on their experimental establishments in Germany. The first weapons were launched against London from sites in northern France shortly after the Allies landed in Normandy, and continued for several months until these were overrun or flattened by the heavy air attacks mounted against them. There followed another phase at the end of 1944 in which the bombs were launched from the air by Heinkel He 111s of KG 3 'Blitz' and KG 53 'Legion Cóndor' (although one such raid had been carried out against Southampton as early as 7 July). With one of these unwieldy weapons carried under the wing root, the He 111 proved to be exceedingly vulnerable and these flying-bomb carriers suffered heavy casualties from the guns of de Havilland Mosquito night-fighters. By the end of the war some 30,000 flying-bombs had been produced, of which 2,400 hit London and a similar number fell on Antwerp; around 5,000 others struck areas in England, France, Belgium and the Netherlands.

Birth of the jet fighter

As the flying-bomb 'offensive' reached its climax in September 1944, examples of Hitler's second terror weapon, the A4 (or V2) rocket missile, were beginning to fall in southern England. These weapons, the first in the era of ballistic missiles, were launched from sites in the Netherlands and, carrying a warhead of some 2,149 lb (975 kg), fell to earth some 200 miles (320 km) distant. Around

As the Allied armies overran the V-1 launching sites the Luftwaffe resorted to carrying the weapons beneath Heinkel He 111s. An He 111H-22 of I/KG 53 with a flying bomb under its starboard wing root is seen here being inspected by German officials in October 1944.

The world's first aircraft to fly purely on turbojet power was the Heinkel He 178; its first true flight took place at Marienehe on 27 August 1939 with Flugkapitän Erich Warsitz at the controls.

6,000 V2s were produced, of which 1,054 fell in the UK and 1,675 on the Continent. Although they, and the flying-bombs, were unpleasant but forlorn attempts to discourage the Allies in their war aims, they nevertheless represented only the spearhead of other substantial research work that was being undertaken on other devastating weapons, which would almost certainly have been used had the Allied invasion of Europe been delayed beyond mid-1944.

As it was, the Allied air attacks on the V1 and V2 (*Vergeltungswaffe* 1 and 2, or Retaliation Weapons 1 and 2) launch sites proved only a short respite from the devastating raids on German cities, and it was to counter these that greatest effort was now made by the Luftwaffe, a phase generally referred to as the Defence of the Reich. But for the intervention by Hitler himself, the most effective fighter that could have significantly blunted the Allied air attacks on Germany (particularly by day) was the Messerschmitt Me 262 jet-propelled fighter and also, given time, the Messerschmitt Me 163 rocket interceptor.

Germany had been hard at work since before the war to develop a turbojet engine, and had indeed flown a research jet aircraft, the Heinkel He 178, on 27 August 1939. Various jet prototypes had flown since, including the Heinkel He 280 twin-jet fighter, but it was the Me 262 which was destined to become the world's first combat jet fighter. Powered by two 1,862-lb (840-kg) thrust Junkers 109-004A turbojets, this aircraft had first flown on 18 July 1942 and before long Hitler was insisting that it should be developed as a fast bomber. By mid-1944 about 25 prototypes and development aircraft had been completed before Hitler reluctantly sanctioned the development of fighter versions. By the end of the year the first operational units had been formed, including JG 7 'Nowotny' (with fighters) and IV/KG 51 'Edelweiss' (with bombers). Casualties were at first high, a consequence of hurried development and training, but gradually the Me 262 was recognized by

The first flight by a jet-powered aircraft designed from the outset as a fighter was made by the Heinkel He 280V1, seen here during that flight on 2 April 1941 with Fritz Schäfer at the controls; the He 280 did not however reach production.

Messerschmitt Me 262

History and Notes

The Messerschmitt Me 262 was the world's first turbojet-powered aircraft to achieve combat status, and was the result of pre-war research with gas turbines in Germany. Design of the aircraft started in 1938 and prototype airframes were ready in 1941 but, as the Junkers jet engines were not then ready, the first flight on 18 April was made using a single Jumo 210G piston engine; it was not until 18 July 1942 that the Me 262 V3 first made an all-jet flight powered by two 1,852-lb (840-kg) thrust Junkers 109-004A-0 turbojets. Early prototypes featured tailwheel landing gear, but when production started in 1944 a tricycle arrangement had been standardized. As Hitler persisted in demanding development of the Me 262 as a bomber for reprisal raids on the UK, development of the fighter was badly delayed and it was not until late in 1944 that the aircraft entered Luftwaffe service. The Me 262A-1a Schwalbe (Swallow) fighter was armed with four 30-mm guns in the nose and joined Kommando Nowotny in October; it was followed by the Me 262A-1a/U1 with two additional 20-mm guns, the Me 262 A-1a/U2 bad-weather fighter and the Me 262A-1a/U3 unarmed reconnaissance aircraft. The Me 262A-2a Sturmvogel (Stormy Petrel) bomber could carry up to 2,205 lb (1000 kg) of bombs in addition to the four 30-mm guns, and a two-seat version (with prone bomb aim-

er), the Me 262A-2a/U2, was also produced.

Before the end of the war Me 262s were being flown with some success against Allied bombers both as day and night fighters (the latter were radar-equipped Me 262B-1a/U1s), and air-to-air rockets were being developed. Dogged by difficulties brought on by Allied raids on factories and airfields, the Luftwaffe's jet fighter units nevertheless posed a formidable threat to Allied air superiority during the last few months of the war.

Specification: Messerschmitt Me 262A-1a
Origin: Germany
Type: single-seat interceptor fighter
Powerplant: two 1,984-lb (900-kg) thrust Junkers Jumo 109-004B-4 turbojets

Performance: maximum speed 541 mph (870 km/h) at 22,965 ft (7000 m); initial climb rate 3,937 ft (1200 m) per minute; service ceiling 36,090 ft (11000 m); normal range 525 miles (845 km)
Weights: empty 8,818 lb (4000 kg); maximum take-off 14,936 lb (6775 kg)
Dimensions: span 41 ft 0⅛ in (12.50 m); length 34 ft 9½ in (10.61 m); height 12 ft 6¾ in (3.83 m); wing area 233.3 sq ft (21.68 m²)
Armament: four 30-mm MK 108 cannon in nose

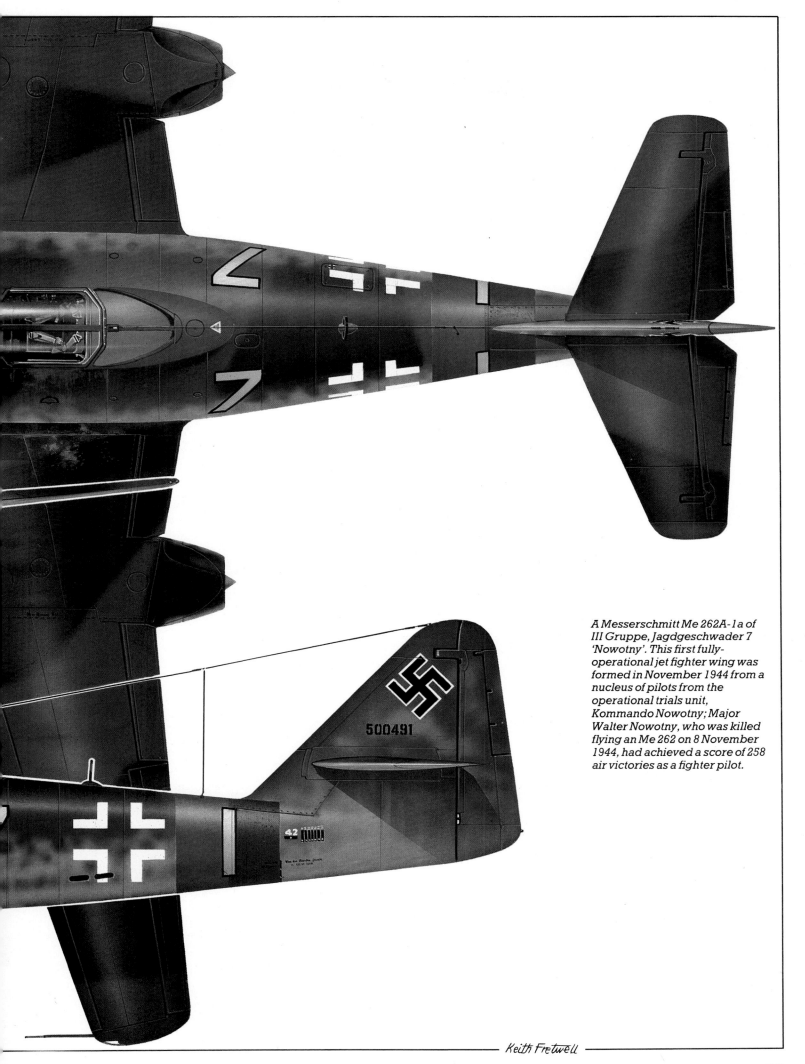

A Messerschmitt Me 262A-1a of III Gruppe, Jagdgeschwader 7 'Nowotny'. This first fully-operational jet fighter wing was formed in November 1944 from a nucleus of pilots from the operational trials unit, Kommando Nowotny; Major Walter Nowotny, who was killed flying an Me 262 on 8 November 1944, had achieved a score of 258 air victories as a fighter pilot.

Keith Fretwell

The Messerschmitt Me 262A-1a/
U3 was a reconnaissance version
equipped with two vertical Rb50/
30 cameras; this example served
on Einsatzkommando Braunegg
in Northern Italy in March 1945.
Oberleutnant Herward
Braunegg was a reconnaissance
pilot who had won the Knight's
Cross in April 1944.

Messerschmitt Me 262-1a

1 Flettner-type geared trim
   tab
2 Mass-balanced rudder
3 Rudder post
4 Tail fin structure
5 Tailplane structure
6 Rudder tab mechanism
7 Flettner-type servo tab
8 Starboard elevator
9 Rear navigation light
10 Rudder linkage
11 Elevator linkage
12 Tailplane adjustment
   mechanism

13 Fuselage break point
14 Fuselage construction
15 Control runs
16 FuG 25a loop antenna (IFF)
17 Automatic compass
18 Aft auxiliary self-sealing
   fuel tank (132 imp gal/600
   litre capacity)
19 FuG 16zy R/T
20 Fuel filler cap
21 Aft cockpit glazing
22 Armoured aft main fuel
   tank (198 Imp gal/900 litre
   capacity)

23 Inner cockpit shell
24 Pilot's seat
25 Canopy jettison lever
26 Armoured (15-mm) head
   rest
27 Canopy (hinged to
   starboard)
28 Canopy lock
29 Bar-mounted Revi 16B
   sight (for both cannon and
   R4M missiles)
30 Armourglass windscreen
   (90-mm)
31 Instrument panel

Although better remembered as
a fighter, the Me 262 was initially
developed as a bomber (at
Hitler's personal insistence);
carrying a pair of 1,102-lb (500-
kg) bombs, this Me 262A-2a was
flown by 1./KG 51 'Edelweiss' in
March 1945.

Here shown bearing the full
codes, 9K+FH, this Me 262A-2a
of 1./KG 51 'Edelweiss' was
based at Achmer in the last
weeks of the war. Shortage of
fuel eventually grounded this
unit and its surviving aircraft
were captured intact by the
advancing Allies.

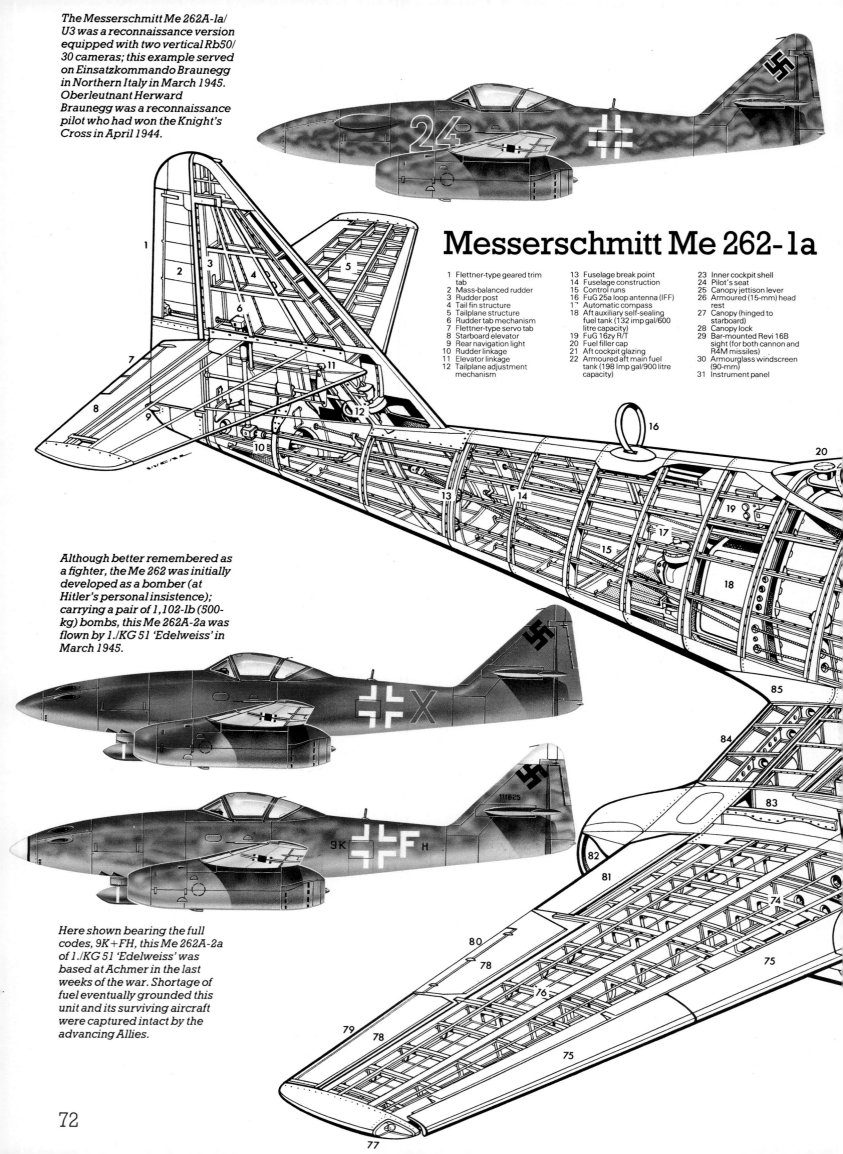

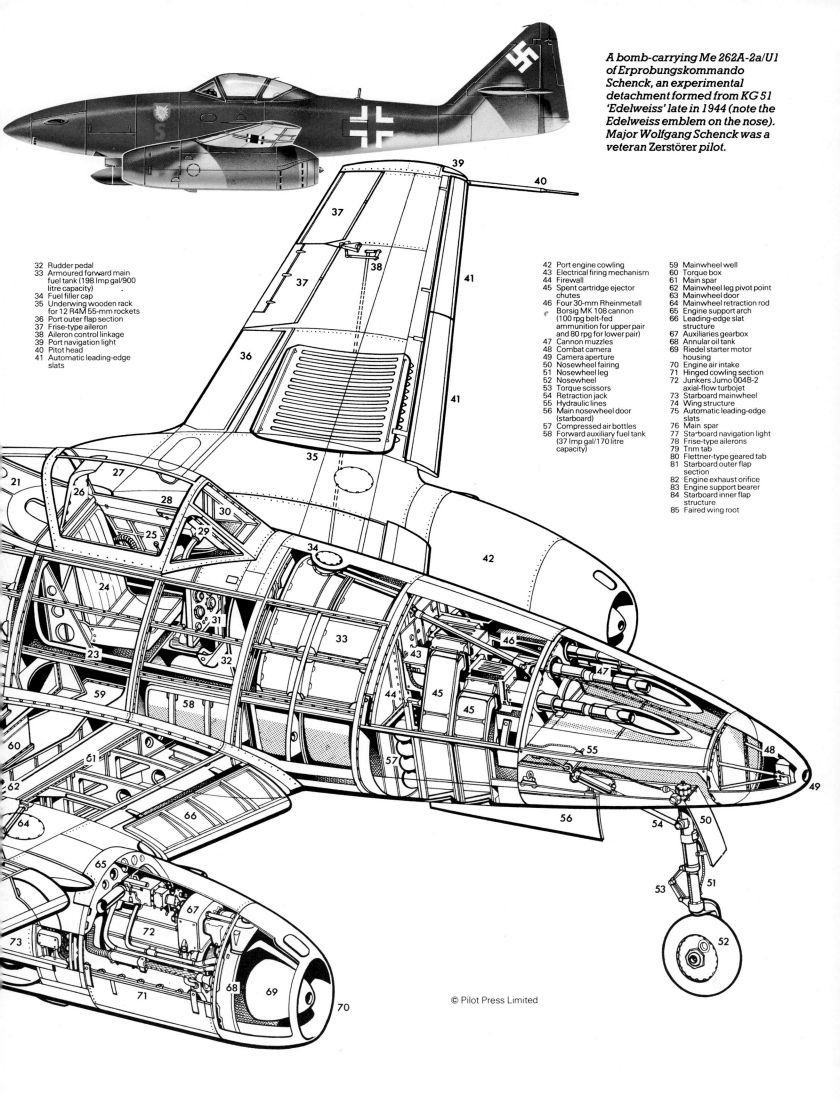

A bomb-carrying Me 262A-2a/U1 of Erprobungskommando Schenck, an experimental detachment formed from KG 51 'Edelweiss' late in 1944 (note the Edelweiss emblem on the nose). Major Wolfgang Schenck was a veteran Zerstörer pilot.

32 Rudder pedal
33 Armoured forward main fuel tank (198 Imp gal/900 litre capacity)
34 Fuel filler cap
35 Underwing wooden rack for 12 R4M 55-mm rockets
36 Port outer flap section
37 Frise-type aileron
38 Aileron control linkage
39 Port navigation light
40 Pitot head
41 Automatic leading-edge slats

42 Port engine cowling
43 Electrical firing mechanism
44 Firewall
45 Spent cartridge ejector chutes
46 Four 30-mm Rheinmetall Borsig MK 108 cannon (100 rpg belt-fed ammunition for upper pair and 80 rpg for lower pair)
47 Cannon muzzles
48 Combat camera
49 Camera aperture
50 Nosewheel fairing
51 Nosewheel leg
52 Nosewheel
53 Torque scissors
54 Retraction jack
55 Hydraulic lines
56 Main nosewheel door (starboard)
57 Compressed air bottles
58 Forward auxiliary fuel tank (37 Imp gal/170 litre capacity)

59 Mainwheel well
60 Torque box
61 Main spar
62 Mainwheel leg pivot point
63 Mainwheel door
64 Mainwheel retraction rod
65 Engine support arch
66 Leading-edge slat structure
67 Auxiliaries gearbox
68 Annular oil tank
69 Riedel starter motor housing
70 Engine air intake
71 Hinged cowling section
72 Junkers Jumo 004B-2 axial-flow turbojet
73 Starboard mainwheel
74 Wing structure
75 Automatic leading-edge slats
76 Main spar
77 Starboard navigation light
78 Frise-type ailerons
79 Trim tab
80 Flettner-type geared tab
81 Starboard outer flap section
82 Engine exhaust orifice
83 Engine support bearer
84 Starboard inner flap structure
85 Faired wing root

© Pilot Press Limited

73

the Allies as being a dangerous new opponent with its speed of 536 mph (868 km/h) and armament of four 30-mm cannon. During the last four months of the war a new unit, Jagdverband 44 (staffed by some of the best fighter pilots of the Luftwaffe and led by General Adolf Galland), was equipped with Me 262s and in the space of a month, during which seldom more than six aircraft were available, destroyed at least 45 Allied aircraft. Me 262s were also delivered to a number of bomber units whose personnel received hurried training as fighter pilots, including KG(J)/6, KG(J)/27 and I KG(J)/54. Other Me 262s (the Me 262B-1a/U1) were developed and used operationally as two-seat radar-equipped night-fighters in the defence of Berlin.

A Messerschmitt Me 262B-1a/U1 two-seat jet night fighter with Lichtenstein SN-2 radar; aircraft of this type were flown by Kommando Welter in defence of Berlin during March 1945. The aircraft shown here carries markings applied after capture by the Allies.

Technical advances

Another aircraft that entered service as a jet bomber was the twin-jet Arado Ar 234 Blitz (Lightning) and this equipped KG 76 during the last three months of the war. Its top speed of 461 mph (742 km/h) rendered it almost immune from interception by Allied fighters and there were plans to introduce a four-jet version, the Ar 234C; a night-fighter version did, however, just see service before the end of the war.

An Arado Ar 234B Blitz twin-jet bomber. A photo reconnaissance version served with 1. Versuchsverband Oberbefehlshaber der Luftwaffe in 1944 and flew numerous high altitude photo sorties over Britain, being wholly immune from interception by Allied fighters.

An Arado Ar 234B-2 of 9./KG 76, commanded by Major Hans-Georg Bätcher and based at Rheine and Achmer. II/KG 76 became fully operational in February 1945, losing its first aircraft in action on the 24th with P-47s near Segelsdorf.

Messerschmitt Me 163

History and Notes

The Messerschmitt Me 163 Komet (Comet) rocket interceptor stemmed from prolonged research by Dr Alexander Lippisch over 15 years before the war. The prototype was initially test flown as a glider during the spring of 1941 before being fitted with a Walter RII-203 rocket using *T-Stoff* and *Z-Stoff* propellants. Powered flights by the Me 163 V1 started in the late summer of 1941, and on 2 October the aircraft reached 623.8 mph (1004.5 km/h); two months later the Me 163B Komet was ordered into production.

Production Me 163Bs were powered by Walter 109-509A rocket motors using *T-Stoff* (hydrogen peroxide) and *C-Stoff* (hydrazine hydrate, methyl alcohol and water) to give a thrust of 3,748 lb (1700 kg). Early Me 163B-0s were armed with a pair of 20-mm guns, but Me 163 B-1s carried two 30-mm weapons. The aircraft possessed no conventional landing gear, but took off from a trolley which was jettisoned immediately after take-off.

Introduction to Luftwaffe service was a protracted and hazardous process owing to difficulties in handling the fuels and a number of fatal accidents, and only very experienced pilots were selected. Production Me 163B-1a fighters equipped I./JG 400 at Brandis, near Leipzig, in June 1944 and first intercepted B-17 Fortress daylight bombers on 16 August that year. All manner of difficulties faced the pilots, apart from the hazards already mentioned, and it was found difficult to aim and fire the guns with the result that upward-firing 50-mm shells and underwing rockets came to be developed.

Although some 300 Me 163Bs were produced (as well as a few Me 163Cs with increased fuel) and JG 400's other two *Gruppen* re-equipped by the end of 1944, only nine confirmed air victories were achieved by the *Geschwader*.

Specification: Messerschmitt Me 163B-1a Komet
Origin: Germany

The Messerschmitt Me 163B-1 Komet rocket interceptor suffered all the problems of radical design in conditions of overwhelming chaos and privation in late-war Germany.

Type: single-seat interceptor fighter
Powerplant: one 3,748-lb (1700-kg) thrust Walter 109-509A-2 rocket motor
Performance: maximum speed 596 mph (960 km/h) at 9,845 ft (3000 m); initial climb rate 11,810 ft (3600 m) per minute; service ceiling 39,700 ft (12100 m); normal range 50 miles (80 km)
Weights: empty 4,200 lb (1905 kg); maximum take-off 9,061 lb (4110 kg)
Dimensions: span 30 ft 7¼ in (9.33 m); length 18 ft 8 in (5.69 m); height 9 ft 0½ in (2.76 m); wing area 211.2 sq ft (19.62 m²)
Armament: two 30-mm MK 108 cannon

Messerschmitt Me 163B

Operational Me 163B-1 Komets of Jagdgeschwader 400, the only combat unit to fly the extraordinary little fighter.

An even more imaginative interceptor was the Messerschmitt Me 163 Komet rocket aircraft which started to equip a special fighter unit, JG 400, in mid-1944 near Leipzig. This extraordinary little aircraft, with a top speed of 596 mph (960 km/h), an armament of two 30-mm cannon and an endurance of only 8 minutes under full power, was dogged by handling hazards with its extremely sensitive rocket fuels, and many pilots lost their lives in shattering explosions on the ground following fuel leakage. However, although some 300 Komets were produced, they destroyed fewer than a dozen enemy aircraft. Certainly no Allied fighter could match them in air combat.

One other expedient in air defence is worth mentioning here, the small single-jet Heinkel He 162 'Volksjäger' (or People's Fighter), or Salamander as it was often termed. It was a single-seat aircraft built largely of wood for ease and speed of production and mounted its BMW 109-003 engine on top of the fuselage behind the cockpit. With an armament of two 30-mm cannon, He 162s were issued to Einsatzkommando Bär (commanded by Oberst Heinz Bär, a pilot who gained 220 air victories during the war) and later to JG 1, and by the end of the war about 275 aircraft had been flown and a further 800 were nearing completion.

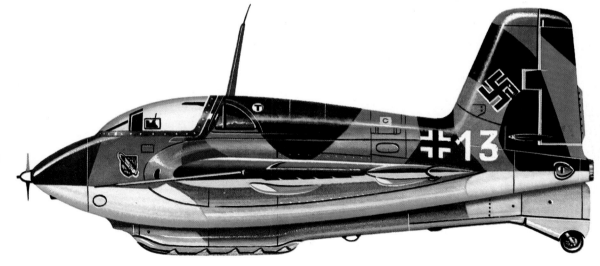

This Me 163B-1 wears the Geschwaderzeichen of JG 400; the badge displays a rocket-powered flea and the words 'Wie ein Floh, aber Oho!' (Only a flea, but Oh-Oh!). The prominent 'T' and 'C' stencils on the aircraft indicated fuelling points for the two liquid fuels, accidental contact between which would result in catastrophe.

German Warplanes of World War II

Despite its hurried development, the ingenious Heinkel He 162 would have proved an effective fighter in experienced hands, but there was insufficient time remaining for the Luftwaffe to assemble and train men of the calibre required.

An He 162A-2 of II Gruppe, Jagdgeschwader 1, which was captured by the Allies at Leck on 8 May 1945. This machine is currently stored at RAF St Athan.

Front view of a Heinkel He 162 emphasizes the radical concept of this small fighter, in particular the location of the turbojet, the narrow-track undercarriage and the sharply angled-down wing tips – the latter found necessary to improve stability in high-g turns.

A Heinkel He 162 in flight. Despite enormous administrative effort, mass production of this largely wooden fighter (whose production target was 4,000 aircraft a month by May 1945) fell steadily behind schedule, and by the end of the war only about 275 were completed.

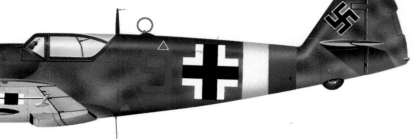

Displaying a green 'Defence of the Reich' fuselage band, this Messerschmitt Bf 109K-4 served with I Gruppe, Jagdgeschwader 27 at Rheine in December 1944. The application of the 'Afrika' badge, reminiscent of happier hunting by JG 27 in 1941, is somewhat ironic.

Another Bf 109K-4, this time of II Gruppe, Jagdgeschwader 77, based at Bönninghardt in December 1944, and sporting a green and white fuselage band. An obvious feature of this version was the 'Galland' hood with reduced framing – originally introduced in the 'Gustav'.

While these advanced aircraft were evidence of Germany's enormous technological potential, the chaotic conditions brought about by shortage of materials and destruction of her research and manufacturing facilities ensured greater dependence upon established aircraft, albeit aircraft with considerable improvement.

The splendid Messerschmitt Bf 109G had been joined in service by the Bf 109K with boosted DB 605D engine, the Bf 109K-4 having a top speed of 452 mph (728 km/h) and the Bf 109K-6 an armament of three 30-mm and two 13-mm (0.51-in) guns. As a macabre postscript to this superb fighter, the final operation which it fought during the war was by Rammkommando Elbe on 7 April 1945, when 120 Bf 109s took off to ram American bombers in an approaching raid; only 15 returned.

End of the line

The Focke-Wulf Fw 190 appeared in much developed form during the autumn of 1944 with a boosted Jumo 213A inline engine in lengthened radial-type cowling. This version, the 'long-nose' Fw 190D (of which the Fw 190D-9, or 'Dora-Nine', was the most widely used) had a top speed of 426

The Dornier Do 335 twin tandem engine bomber was just beginning to appear in numbers at the end of the war. Potentially the fastest piston-engine aircraft ever built, early versions had a top speed of 474 mph (763 km/h) but just failed to reach operational status, although a few were sighted in the air by Allied fighter pilots.

Prototype for the Focke-Wulf Fw 190 'Dora' series was the Fw 190 V53, powered by a Jumo 213A inline engine in annular cowling. Armament was four 20-mm wing guns and two 13-mm (0.51-m) guns in the nose.

mph (685 km/h) and was certainly a match for any Allied fighter. Large numbers of Fw 190D-9s were completed but, like so many other operations, dire shortages of fuel kept most of them grounded during the final desperate weeks of the Defence of the Reich. This was generally regarded as the best of all Germany's piston-engined fighters of the war, and was the progenitor of Kurt Tank's Ta 152, an excellent high-altitude fighter with a top speed of 472 mph (760 km/h) at over 41,010 ft (12500 m), which was just reaching fighter units at the end of the war.

Desperate measures

The appalling losses suffered by the Luftwaffe's *Kampfgeschwader* in 1943-4, their redeployment in other roles and the priority eventually bestowed on fighter production all contributed to the demise of the German bomber force towards the end of the war, and the last quasi-strategic operations by Germany's true heavy bomber (the Heinkel He 177) were those by KG 1 on the Russian front in June and July 1944, but it was the general shortage of fuel as much as Soviet fighter opposition that finally brought an end to these operations.

Instead the Luftwaffe undertook the use of yet another extraordinary weapon, the *Mistel* (Mistletoe) composite weapon, involving the mounting of a manned single-seat fighter (usually a Bf 109 or Fw 190) on the top of an explosive-packed Junkers Ju 88. The composite weapon was flown to the

Opposite, bottom: Only version of the Focke-Wulf Ta 152 to reach combat status was the Ta 152H-1, for which the Ta 152 V5, seen here on compass platform, served as prototype. Top speed of this version was 472 mph (760 km/h) at 41,000 ft (12497 m).

Powered by a DB 603G driving a huge four-blade propeller, the high altitude Fw 190 V18 was intended as prototype for the proposed Fw 190 C-series. Equipped with turbo-supercharger and pressure cabin, this aircraft was said to have had a top speed of slightly over 480 mph (772 km/h).

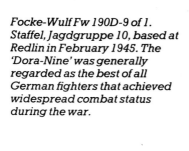

Focke-Wulf Fw 190D-9 of 1. Staffel, Jagdgruppe 10, based at Redlin in February 1945. The 'Dora-Nine' was generally regarded as the best of all German fighters that achieved widespread combat status during the war.

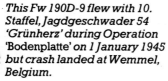

This Fw 190D-9 flew with 10. Staffel, Jagdgeschwader 54 'Grünherz' during Operation 'Bodenplatte' on 1 January 1945 but crash landed at Wemmel, Belgium.

A Focke-Wulf Fw 190D-9 of II Gruppe, Jagdgeschwader 26 'Schlageter', based at Nordhorn in January 1945. The centreline rack shown on this aircraft was for a 66-gal (300-litre) drop tank. II/JG 26 was commanded at that time by Major Anton Hackl.

Displaying black-white-black Defence of the Reich fuselage bands, denoting JG 4, this Fw 190D-9 belonged to the Geschwaderstab and was based at Babenhausen early in 1945.

A 'Dora-Nine' of III Gruppe, Jagdgeschwader 2 'Richthofen', which flew from Altenstadt in December 1944. JG 2 was then commanded by Oberst Kurt Bühligen, holder of the Swords and Oak Leaves, and a pilot with 112 air combat victories.

An operational sortie by Mistel 1 combinations (Junkers Ju 88A-4 and Messerschmitt Bf 109F-1) being prepared, probably at the end of 1944. This extraordinary weapon was flown on numerous occasions in action by Kampfgeschwader 200.

target area where the Ju 88 was released and radio-controlled by the fighter pilot to strike its objective. During the final months of the war numerous *Mistel* attacks were launched (but one against the Scapa Flow naval base was not) with considerable success, particularly against targets behind the swiftly advancing Russian forces.

When the curtain finally fell on Germany in May 1945 the once-vaunted Luftwaffe was a spent force, its better pilots dead and replaced by inadequate tyros, its bases in ruins, the aircraft factories destroyed or captured and its aircraft grounded by lack of fuel. Yet in six years of war its aircrew and aeroplanes had matched anything the Allies had thrown against them until overwhelmed by sheer numbers and weight of bombs. No sensible Allied air commander was ever so foolish as to underestimate the professionalism of the German airman or the ingenuity of German industry and dedication.

A Mistel 1 weapon, probably belonging to 5. (Beleuchter) Staffel, Kampfgeschwader 200, in December 1944. Recent research suggests that over 180 Mistel attacks were flown in the last 10 months of the war.